I0192115

Jamie's Muse

A NOVEL BY

by Bonnie Lee Black

Jamie's Muse
© 2018, Bonnie Lee Black
(www.bonnieleeblack.com)

All rights reserved.

No part of this publication may be reproduced or transmitted in any form or by any means, electronic or mechanical, including photocopying, recording, or any other information storage and retrieval system, without the written permission of the publisher.

Cover image: "Helen of Troy," Dante Gabriel Rossetti (1863)
Author photo: Nancy Anchors
Design: Final Eyes, Taos, New Mexico

Published by Nighthawk Press.
Printed in the United States of America.

ISBN: 978-0-9986807-3-6
Library of Congress Control Number: 2018942997

Other books by Bonnie Lee Black:
Somewhere Child, Viking Press, New York, 1981
How to Cook a Crocodile, Peace Corps Writers, 2010
How to Make an African Quilt, Nighthawk Press,
    Taos, New Mexico, 2013

NIGHTHAWK PRESS
TAOS, NEW MEXICO

Jamie's Muse

to my great-grandchildren

not yet named

The only ghosts, I believe, who creep
into this world, are dead young mothers,
returning to see how their children fare.
There is no other inducement great
enough to bring the dead back.

—J. M. BARRIE, *The Little White Bird*

Helen's Choice

The day I died I was faced with a choice — either run with my son to safety, as my husband was begging me to do, or go to my husband's defense. I chose to pick up my husband's rifle, stand on our veranda, and take aim at his attackers. I shot one, but the others overpowered me. My husband and I died that day in front of our home in Natal. Miraculously, our child's life was spared.

In all these years — both a day and an eternity to the dead, but over a century-and-a-quarter to the living — my soul has not been at peace. Unanswered questions give me no rest: Did I make the right choice? Was it hubris to think I could protect my husband against those men? Should I have obeyed Will and run with our wee babe in my arms in the opposite direction? Did I abandon our son by putting both of his parents' lives at risk? Should I have never left Scotland for South Africa in the first place?

Will I ever know whether what I did was for the best?

Will my spirit ever rest?

My Quest

She died under mysterious circumstances in her early twenties in Natal, South Africa, about 160 years before I was born. Her name is listed as "unknown" on her only son's — my grandfather's — death certificate dated October 31, 1954. But in recent years I've come to realize that the appellation "unknown" simply will not do. I've felt haunted by her. She has become my own, insistent, muse.

I've learned that her full married name was Helen David Black. She was the mother of my father's father. According to my research in Edinburgh, my great-grandmother Helen was born Helen Reid David on May 3, 1862, at 8 p.m. in the hamlet of Southmuir, nestled beside the ancient town of Kirriemuir, overlooking the fertile valley of Strathmore in Angus, Scotland, about five hundred miles north of London.

Helen was born two years, almost to the day, after the town's most celebrated son, novelist and playwright James Matthew Barrie. J. M. ("Jamie") Barrie affectionately referred to his beloved hometown, with its irregularly built, rust-colored sandstone cottages sitting shoulder to shoulder along narrow, winding roads, as his "wee red toony."

As soon as I learned that everyone on my Scottish grandfather's side whom I'd managed to track down in my online research came from Kirriemuir, I was determined to travel there right away. As far as I knew, I was the only one of Helen's fewer-than-two-dozen living American descendants to do so, the only fellow Taurus, fellow adventurer, and fellow Africaphile in the whole, small, fragmented, far-flung family. I felt like the chosen one.

To me, alone among her descendants, Helen of Kirriemuir has taken on mythic proportions. She's become my Helen of Troy, launching my journey across the oceans and through the murky seas of history books into her past.

Even the famous painting of Helen of Troy by Dante Rossetti speaks to me: *Yes,* I think, *that's my Helen's image — her face, her hair, her hands.* In lieu of a photograph of her, I cling to this painting. I read her story in it, noting the blaze behind her. It confirms for me that her life, her youth and beauty, ended in fire.

After five years lived in Africa, I returned to the United States in 2001. Helen never returned to Scotland. For years I've felt her urging me to write the story of her life and death, even if I must draw her story mostly from my own vivid imagination. This journey has become my quest.

Scotland, Summer 2011

In Waverley Station in the center of Edinburgh, I board an East Coast Scot Rail train, which will take me to Dundee. From there I'll take a bus north, to Forfar, then another bus to Kirriemuir. I've made no prior arrangements, no hotel reservations. I'm not even sure there is a hotel in Kirriemuir. But I'm not worried. I feel led, as if by the hand.

I take snapshot-like notes from the clear window of this clean, modern express train as the countryside whizzes by:

Huge, clear-blue sky. Dazzlingly bright, sunny day. *(No rain?)* Open, softly undulating, green-green fields. *(Oats? Barley?)* Clumps of fat, round, deciduous trees, like dark polka dots on an emerald-green dress. White, black, and brown cows enjoying a siesta on the sunny slopes. Sheep grazing near a weathered wooden fence. *(There are more sheep in Scotland than people, I've read.)* An old, stone farmhouse in the foreground. Smooth, rolling hills in the far distance.

My heart is beating hard and fast now in anticipation. *(Soon, soon…)* Some part of me feels as if I'm
coming home.

The local bus from Forfar to Kirriemuir is filled with
friendly gray-haired pensioners dressed in woolen
clothes, as though this were already Autumn. They have
obviously long since given up driving their own cars and
are happy to be chauffeured to their destinations. They
chat animatedly among themselves like old friends,
which they likely are.

Along the way, the old woman sitting behind me
taps my shoulder.

"Excuse me," she says sweetly. "You're taking so
many notes. I thought you might be J. K. Rowling. You
resemble her."

"I wish!" I say, and we smile at each other as the
bus begins to pull to a stop and I get up to leave.

There is, in fact, one hotel in Kirriemuir, called
The Thrums — Thrums being the fictitious name Jamie
Barrie gave his hometown whenever he wrote about
it, as well as the actual name for the loose threads that
dangled from linen-weavers' looms, used for repairing
faults. The bus driver pointed the hotel out to me when
the bus came to a stop near the town square, where a
child-size bronze statue of Barrie's most famous fictitious character, Peter Pan, playing his pipe, stands on a
tall pedestal, taking pride of place.

"Just go down Bank Street here on the right," the woman bus driver gestured as I exited the bus. "It'll be on your left at the end. You can't miss it. Enjoy Kirrie!" she said, using the town's nickname. She smiled and nodded at me, as if admiring the pluck of this not-so-young, solo American adventurer.

I paused for a moment at the base of this central statue and reflected on the magical, mythical, timeless powers of this eternal little boy. For over a hundred years, all over the world, the story of Peter Pan has captivated countless children and adults alike. Was there a family anywhere, especially in English-speaking countries, who didn't know the name Peter Pan?

I recalled that when I was a child, my first, cherished puppet was a Peter Pan marionette. By pulling his strings, I brought him to life. I made him fly! I was his voice! And many decades later, when I bought a Peter Pan costume for my then four-year-old grandson Thomas's first real Halloween, he insisted on wearing it every day for many months afterward, until he outgrew it, and he demanded that we all call him "Peter."

Following the bus driver's directions, I pulled my suitcase-on-wheels down Bank Street to The Thrums. The people at The Thrums, a well-maintained old establishment, known in Helen's day as the Temperance Hotel, then owned by the Scottish Temperance League, smiled when they saw me too. I was their sole hotel guest. Most of today's business, I could see, came from the customers sitting at the bar.

Instead of succumbing to the longing to stretch out on the tartan-draped, queen-size bed in my spacious hotel room, I headed straight for the Tourist Information office on the ground floor of the Gateway to the Glens Museum in Kirrie's town square, where a helpful woman gave me some maps and brochures and pointed out a few places of interest within walking distance. Then, since I'd been too rushed and nervous to eat anything all day, I was drawn to the local bakery — as pretty as a Parisian patisserie — where, after some difficult deliberation, I chose a Forfar Bridie.

One bite of this savory ground-meat-and-onion-filled puff-pastry turnover — Scotland's improved-upon version of England's Cornish pasty — flooded my mind with memories. To please my father and honor his Scottish heritage, my mother had made bridies at home from time to time when I was a child growing up in suburban New Jersey. I'd even tried making them myself in recent years, as Helen's spirit has called to me. This one, which I ate in hand while walking up a road called The Roods in Helen's hometown, was the real thing, made at the source, the bakery clerk told me, in nearby Forfar, where it was first created in the early-to-mid-nineteenth century.

Along The Roods I discovered a narrow, well-worn footpath leading to the Hill of Kirriemuir, where the vast Hill Cemetery stretches. I stopped frequently along this steep pathway to take in the glorious view — one of the most beautiful views in all of Scotland, my tourist brochure claimed — and preserve it in my mind. At one point I pocketed a golf-ball-size chunk of red sandstone (the same red sandstone used to make most of the cottages in this "wee red" town) from a crumbling old retaining wall, figuring no one in Kirrie would miss it.

Standing at the town's highest point in the Hill Cemetery overlooking the horizon-wide, green, undulating valley on that clear, summer afternoon, I felt I could see to the end of the world. The tourist brochure in my hand said that on a clear day from this high point one can see as far as Ben Lui, a hill 72 miles away. But what I really wanted was to see into the past. I wanted to know why my paternal great-grandparents ever left such a beautiful, tranquil place. Both of them were schooled (Scotland was proud of its strong emphasis on education for both boys and girls, even in Helen's day), and presumably intelligent. Neither of them, I felt certain, was hungry, homeless, unlawful or desperate. Why did they feel they had to leave?

The names I noted as I walked among the hundreds of granite, sandstone, and marble headstones had a familiar ring to my American ears, thanks to the Scottish diaspora: Janet Burns, Alexander Smith, William Clark, Helen Scott, Alfred Campbell, Ian Shaw, William Kidd, John Lamont, James McFarlane, Abe Guthrie, Dorothy Maclean, Jeannie Fairweather, John Robb, Cameron Lawson, Jessie Prentice, William Lindsay, Donald Ferguson, David Smith…

Somewhere in that sprawling, hilltop cemetery, Helen's parents, my great-*great*-grandparents, and her only sibling, a younger brother, might be buried, resting in peace with the rest of the town's long-deceased inhabitants and, I hoped, enjoying the breathtaking, panoramic, valley view. But Helen David Black and her husband William Black's names would not be found here, I knew. They'd left their hometown as young newlyweds and sailed to Natal, South Africa, where they met their deaths. The records of their lives end with their wedding in Kirriemuir. The records of their deaths do not exist.

As I wandered among the headstones I felt like a lost soul, filled with incessant, unanswerable questions. I thought of Helen: Why did she agree to leave what to me, at least at first glance, seemed to be a perfectly charming, friendly, and beautiful little Scottish town, in order to emigrate to Africa? At that time, in the early 1880s, Africa was known only as the Dark Continent because it was so potentially dangerous and shrouded in mystery. What sort of young woman would have been fearless enough to travel there then?

What was she running from — or to? Why did she and William have to die so young, so far away — with no eulogies or proper burial or grave markers — so unmourned and forgotten? What could I do to change that official, unfathomable word, "unknown," where Helen's whole name rightly belonged on my grandfather's death certificate?

As I stopped near J. M. Barrie's grand granite gravestone on Kirriemuir's Hill Cemetery, where he is surrounded by his once-close-knit family, I could almost hear Helen's spirit speak to me: "You must tell my story now, my Bonnie lass. It's time for me."

Although my stay in Kirriemuir — known as Kirrie to the locals — was brief, I was able to see with my own eyes the little town that Helen and Will had known as home and feel with my feet the winding streets they had walked.

I toured Jamie Barrie's childhood home and saw the outbuilding, meant as a washhouse, which Jamie used as his own private theater to put on his first dramatic productions.

I saw where Helen, Will, and Jamie had attended school together and the structure (once a church) where Helen and Will were married.

I saw the Wilkie factory, which still manufactures textiles but no longer linen, where Helen worked for a while and the spot where the railway station, where Will had worked before leaving for South Africa, had been.

I saw the fine house where Jamie Barrie, his parents and his sisters lived when the family's fortunes had improved. And I saw the high window to the room where Jamie wrote whenever he was home.

Did he look down from that window onto the little town and think of his childhood friend, Helen, now so far away? Did he have her in mind when he wrote about the girls in his fictitious town of Thrums? Had she become his muse?

Kirriemuir, Summer 1881

This time when the Wilkie factory foreman came to chastise Helen for singing and dancing when she should have been working, he took a different approach. This time, he decided, he would be cleverer. He would punish all of the girls.

"You're not to get a break for lunch for the rest of the week, *none* of you!" he bellowed over the linen machines' deafening clanging. He waved his thick right arm in the air as though casting a wide net, then pointed a fat forefinger directly at Helen. "And you can thank your friend Miss David for that, aye!"

Helen watched the broad, bent back and wide rump of this man as he walked away. *Men shouldn't be made like that — or be made to be like that,* she thought. *What a wretched role he's forced to play.* She turned to her co-workers, young women she'd known and played with since early childhood, but they angrily turned their faces from her.

There had been many times in their lives when these young women had been jealous of Helen for the outward gifts she'd been given — her captivating face and flowing, radiant hair and long, lithe body; her lovely singing voice and effortless, flawless dancing. It was as if, they'd murmured among themselves, God had taken all the beauty and talent available to one small town and wrapped it into one girl alone, Helen Reid David, leaving the rest of them with everyday, unremarkable ordinariness.

But here at the linen factory in Kirriemuir, Helen's frequent singing and occasional dancing had often entertained them, making the women laugh, breaking the monotony of their long, slow, tedious hours at the clanging machines. They knew *they* would not get in trouble. Only Helen would.

Yes, whenever Helen couldn't bear her factory-captivity any longer, she would break the rules — leave her place in the line, stretch her stiff legs and dance a quick jig, causing the foreman to lumber from his chair to threaten her again. Her co-workers would watch her, smiling, then band together in quiet solidarity to secretly hate the foreman, their common oppressor.

But this time was different. Helen could read this on the young women's angry faces. They'd *all* have no break for lunch for the rest of the week, which meant several days. No time to eat, or sit outside in nice weather and chat among themselves, or walk to Kirriemuir's town square to do family errands. The foreman's shrewd strategy worked. Suddenly, the free-spirited Helen David, whom most of the women had long resented, became their collective enemy.

At the end of that day, feeling physically drained, faint from hunger, and most of all ostracized by her co-workers, Helen left the linen factory, alone, and walked the short distance to the railway station to meet William at his office there. When she told him what had occurred that day, William listened thoughtfully, without judgment. He'd known Helen, whom he liked to call "Hellion," for most of his life. He knew better than to cross swords with her. He loved her for her glow, her fire; and, like fire, he knew she could sometimes smolder, sometimes burn.

"I'm sorry you've had a bad day, Hel," he ventured calmly. "My philosophy is, work is work, and we all have to do it in some form. There's no way around it, my girl. There will be bad days…." He paused, waiting for a possible rebuttal, but it didn't come.

"In my own case, though," he said, trying to find a bright side, "I'm lucky that I love my work. I like that I'm alone in the station much of the time. Between arrivals and departures, when no whistles are blowing and no passengers are demanding answers to questions or buying tickets, it's quiet. I like that. And when my paperwork is done, I even have time to make drawings in my sketchbook. Would you like to see what I drew today?"

She looked up at his handsome face, so open and guileless, and her heart softened. He had a way of changing the subject, turning her mind and her eyes to see the good. Always the good. Despite his beloved mother's death two years before, and his strict father's ceaseless strictures, William always strove to be sunny. Helen smiled at him and reached out her right hand to admire his latest drawing of a locomotive engine.

For the rest of their walk home to Southmuir, up the steep embankment of the broad, green Commonty in the cool, ebbing-summer air, they talked of their late-October wedding plans. It would be a small wedding, just their immediate families — Helen's parents and brother, and Will's father — and their closest friends, held in Southmuir's South Parish Church. After their marriage, they would live "happily ever after — like storybook characters," Helen, still only nineteen and full of romantic dreams, insisted. Her grandest wish was to spend the rest of her life with her tall, strong, steady, sunny Will.

When she opened the front door of her parents' cottage, Helen found her mother at work at the loom in the dimming daylight streaming in from the room's one, low, square window. Helen's gray-haired mother Agnes was, as was her wont, unhappy with her lot and quick to bend Helen's ear.

"Well, aye, I'm glad to set eyes on you, my bonny lass! I've been here, all by mysel' all the day. Your father and brother are god-knows-where as us'al, and I've been home alone workin' my gnarled fingers to the bone. You, at least, get to spend your day in the comp'ny of your friends, workin' on shiny, new-fangled looms. But me, I'm too old and bent now to work in a nice modern factory like you, makin' more money than I ever could at home. Look a' me. What's t' become o' me?"

Helen glanced at her tired old mother, then looked away. She couldn't answer. She had never expressed to Agnes how much she hated working in the Wilkie linen factory, standing all day, from dawn until dusk, five-and-a-half days a week, with all the other sheep-like young women in front of the huge, cold, clanging, deafening steam-powered weaving machines, feeling like she was becoming a machine and losing herself.

Every day that she had to face the wide, white, flat, ever-rolling, never-ending linen fabric she saw it as a screen that separated her from real life. Her mind, heart, and body rebelled. She ground her teeth. Her hands and feet froze. She was forced to dance from time to time to make her chilled blood flow again, to remind herself she was human.

Helen had heard her mother's grievances so many times she'd lost all pity for her.

Her mother "rued the day" she'd met and married Alexander David in 1859. Agnes had been a "proud Kirrie weaver," a childless widow of thirty-five, with a cottage in Southmuir. Alexander, known as Sandy, just twenty-two and "handsome as the devil," Agnes always admitted, was passing through from Dundee, "hungry in ev'ry way." So Agnes took him in, fed him and, soon after, wed him. And she'd regretted it all every day since. "All excep' the two bonny babes he ga' me," Agnes inevitably added with a sad smile.

Helen had grown up watching her mother at work at that same loom, filling the room with the clack and clatter of its flying shuttle and the sturdy, light-brown linen cloth that steadily emerged. Her earliest memory was of her mother fastening her younger brother's cradle by a cord to the loom's treadle to lull the baby to sleep, despite the loom's noise. Because her father was often gone, "god-knows-where," and out of work, Helen's mother's weaving, like that of most of the townsfolk, had been the main support of the family. Helen had always admired her mother for that.

Yes, somewhere in her heart Helen knew she still felt love and admiration for her mother, but for the sake of domestic peace she kept her distance and didn't take sides. When her father was home and sober, he was charming, witty, and good-natured. He told his only daughter often how much he loved his "bonny girl."

Agnes's constantly gloomy moods, on the other hand, like Scotland's weather, fell like cold rain on Helen's soul. Now that her mother was old—nearing sixty—and heavier than ever in both body and spirit, her new refrain had become, "What's t' become o' me?"

What will become of her? Helen wondered as she turned toward the hearth to begin preparing supper. She peeled and cut up some potatoes, covered them with water in a pot, and set the pot on the fire to boil. She took a loaf of brown bread from a shelf and unwrapped a lump of salt butter. She picked a bunch of kale from their kitchen garden, cleaned it in the back washhouse, ripped it roughly and added it to the potatoes for soup. She was hungry and tired, but also tired of potatoes and kale. She made a pot of tea and poured herself a cup.

That Saturday night, Helen and William attended the village dance, as they did most every week. William was a shy, tentative dancer, but he knew that dancing these traditional Scottish country dances gave Helen an important outlet, more so this week than ever.

As everyone in Kirriemuir knew by now, the young Helen David excelled at dancing. When she skipped and kicked and twirled to the fiddlers' fast-tempo reel, she seemed to be on fire. Although it was normally frowned upon to attempt self-glorification in such mixed-group social dancing, older onlookers often encouraged Helen to have the whole floor, and her fellow young dancers, some resentfully, stepped back to watch Helen as well. She held her full skirt up with both hands, exposing the lower half of her long, shapely legs and showing to all that every step of her ghillie-shod feet was perfectly placed and paced to the lively music.

Onlookers agreed among themselves that Helen's poise and technique were impeccable. No one that they could recall had ever danced a reel quite like her. They clapped and whooped as they watched her — the confident tilt of her head, the wildness of her hair, the fire in her eyes, the unbridled joy in her smile.

Some people also begged her to sing at these social gatherings, and she was happy to comply with their wishes. She knew the words of dozens of songs, from church hymns and Scottish ballads to a few bawdy songs she'd learned from traveling minstrels at the town's semiannual Mucklie markets held in the square. That night, when she sang Burns' "Red, Red Rose," she changed his words to "bonny lad" and directed her gaze toward an embarrassed Will:

> … As fair art thou, my bonny lad,
>> So deep in love am I;
> And I will love thee still, my dear,
>> Till a' the seas gang dry.

> … Till a' the seas gang dry, my dear,
>> And the rocks melt wi' the sun,
> And I will love thee still, my dear,
>> While the sands o' life shall run.

Clearly Helen loved being the center of attention and having people look at her with cocked heads, the way art lovers marvel at rare paintings. More even than the attention she received, she loved giving her admirers pleasure. She saw how the village elders' normally tired, weatherworn faces lit up when they watched her dance and sing. She saw the audience's eyes widen and their mouths stretch into smiles. She encouraged them to participate by keeping time — clapping their hands and tapping their feet — as she leapt and twirled, her long hair swirled, and sparks seemed to fly all around her. She tried not to note the angry, envious glances from the plainest young women, her co-workers, in the crowd.

Jamie Barrie, Helen's childhood friend, was too shy to attend Kirrie's social dances and admire Helen there. But he had recognized Helen's theatrical talents early. She had been his chosen "leading lady" in his first theatrical productions staged in the small, whitewashed washhouse behind his family's home on Brechin Road. As a diminutive seven-year-old, he had directed the five-year-old Helen in the role of the fairy queen.

Helen's mother Agnes had made her a fairy queen costume of homespun linen, stiffening the petals and wings with potato starch so they looked as light as air. Jamie told her, "You ARE a fairy queen!" and she *became* the fairy queen of his dreams. He said, "Chin up! Arms up! Dance as if you are flying in thin air!" And so she did. She transformed herself at his command and transported the rapt audience of neighborhood children to the place of Jamie's imagining. She became his willing marionette. *This is magic,* Jamie thought, *and I am the magician!*

In recent years Jamie had often encouraged Helen to pursue a career as an actress in London, but she had dismissed his comments. *Too unrealistic,* she'd thought. Up to this point in her life, Kirriemuir, Angus, was a big enough stage.

The next afternoon, after church, Helen's small family enjoyed a rare, quiet Sunday dinner together at home.

Her father and brother had returned the day before bearing offerings of fresh fish from what they claimed was a fishing trip, and her mother was too grateful for the fish and their safe return to make a fuss. So the four of them ate in peace.

Afterward, Helen paid a visit to the Barries' new home, Strath View, on Glamis Road in Southmuir. She enjoyed visiting this spacious house, with its modern parlor, plush furniture, and enchanting semicircular staircase, almost as much as she'd enjoyed spending time as a young girl at the Barries' smaller first home on Brechin Road. There was always love and harmony here, despite the fact that Margaret Ogilvy, Jamie's mother, had become a near-invalid after Jamie's older brother David died. Margaret was essentially confined to bed now, and those of her children who still lived at home doted on her.

Helen was relieved to see that her childhood friend Jamie was indeed at home, since his studies at Edinburgh University often kept him away. She needed to talk with her old friend, the only person, she felt, who truly understood what she was made of, down deep.

When she told him what had happened at the linen factory that week, he sympathized. "You poor dear!" the small, thin fellow said in his high-pitched voice, genuinely concerned. "How awful! What will you do? Let's go for a walk on this fine day and put our heads together..."

They walked side by side, as they'd done so many times before, along roads rutted by carriage wheels and horses' hooves, away from town, into the undulating valley, in the direction of the distant Grampian hills. Their silhouettes against the sky showed a peculiar pair: she, tall and willowy with her long, loose, honey-colored hair glinting in the afternoon sun, and he, round-shouldered, pencil-thin and only five feet tall, wearing a well worn fishing hat and using a walking stick as if he were a child-size old man. He was only twenty-one.

"That factory," Jamie hissed, "is like a giant that has come to possess our wee red toony, waving his conqueror's flag in the air in the form of smoke from his chimney-stack, and putting the old weavers out of work! Yes, Helen, a new era has dawned! What will it mean for us?"

Normally socially withdrawn, Jamie felt at ease in the company of his first and favorite leading lady. He talked freely and animatedly as Helen walked beside him, listening to him intently, as if he were still her stage director.

"Perhaps there is cause to protest!" Jamie declared with his usual dramatic flare. "My mother often talks about the Weavers' Riot of 1839, when she was a girl, and how Kirrie's weavers — women as well as men — in a dispute over wages, armed with stones and other missiles — including haddock heads! — drove the constables back at every point, until a wild and lawless riot ensued. *Oh, how exciting!* I think I'll write about that event one day…"

His voice trailed off dreamily as if he'd already begun to write that story in his ever-imaginative mind. But Helen soon brought him back to earth. She explained to him that she'd grown to despise "that factory," its tedium and facelessness. She felt trapped, like an animal in a cage — like the caged animals she and Jamie had seen as children in the traveling fairs and shows that came through Kirrie every year. She stopped walking, looked into his deep-set, clear blue eyes imploringly, and asked for his advice. *What could she do? What should she do?*

He wanted to be brave and wise. He wanted to have the answer, to be her hero. He looked up, admiring her face as if it were Beauty incarnate, preserved in oils on canvas. His feelings for her were deep and pure, like the love he felt for his four adoring sisters — Maggie, Isabella, Sara, and Jane Ann — and, of course, his beloved mother: unsullied by physical desire. Helen, he knew, would soon be marrying the tall, handsome William Black; they would share carnal love. But he, James Matthew Barrie, and his dear friend Helen Reid David would always have something better and more enduring — a *soul* connection.

But all he could think to say to her was, "You could always leave, you know." He gestured with his walking stick circling high in the air, "You could fly away, like a bird, or like a fairy queen!"

Helen's stern look brought him down to earth again with a thud.

"Really," he said. "You don't have to stay here. The world is wide. Have you thought about the colonies? I see adverts all the time in the newspapers in Edinburgh. They need people, especially able-bodied young men and women, in the colonies. William would be well qualified to work for the railway somewhere. Shall I clip these adverts when I see them and send them to you?"

Helen's eyes widened and a slow smile crept across her face. She glanced down at her dear, dear friend, whose directions she'd always trusted, and nodded.

Yes. Yes!

Southmuir, Autumn 1881

"God of Abraham and the God of Ruth," Reverend Alexander Duff, minister of the South Parish Church in Southmuir, prayed, "who you asked to trust you and journey with you; you call us to embark on a journey of faith. We stand before you ready to hear your call and to follow wherever you lead…"

William hardly heard a word. Standing in front of the wedding guests, facing his Helen, who looked more like an angel than a hellion in her long white linen dress and lace veil, he was tempted to whisk her away by the hand, to fly away with her, away from all this fuss, this show. But he stood fast, paralyzed with nervousness, trembling in place, trusting that all eyes were on his beautiful bride instead of on him.

He knew he had to be strong for Helen's sake.

"… Through the journey of life, with its many twists and turns," Reverend Duff prayed on, "we long for a straight path where the way ahead is visible and clear…"

William looked down into Helen's blue-green eyes and thought he saw eternity there. He felt as if he were the luckiest man in all of Scotland — no, in all the world

— no, the luckiest man who'd ever lived, the luckiest man in history — to claim her love forever. They would love each other far longer than "as long as you both shall live," he knew. They would love each other "till a' the seas gang dry and the rocks melt wi' the sun." They would love each other for eternity.

"…Gracious God," the minister droned on, "today we support Helen and William, companions on life's road. Look with mercy upon Helen and William, who have come seeking your blessing. Let your Holy Spirit rest upon them so that with steadfast love they may honor the promises they make this day…"

Before Helen and Will made their marriage vows, Reverend Duff asked the gathering for their own vow of support to the young couple.

"Do you, as family and friends of Helen and William pledge your prayerful support and encouragement to the covenant commitment that they are about to make together?"

In one cheerful chorus, the small gathering filling the first few rows of pews at the front of the church, including William's stern father and Helen's disgruntled mother, said a loud, "We DO!"

It seemed that everyone in Southmuir had always felt that Helen and Will were destined for this day. People had even quipped that William Black was "God's Will for our one-and-only Helen David."

It was William's turn to speak, but he wasn't convinced he could. He took a deep breath, cleared his throat, glanced at Helen for courage, and repeated after Reverend Duff: "I, William, take thee, Helen, to be my wedded wife…"

Within minutes, which felt to Will like years, they were married. A bagpiper friend played a joyous recessional. After signing the registry book on that brisk, sunny autumn afternoon, October 28, 1881, when the surrounding flame-hued trees had not yet shed their leaves, Helen and Will were outside of Southmuir's South Parish Church, arm in arm, no longer two people but one husband-and-wife-forever, being congratulated by all. Neighborhood children stopped at the church's gate to gawk and murmur, "Oh, isn't Helen beau-ti-ful!" … "Aye, look wha' a' bonny bride she is!"

William's father, John Black, who was as tall and slim as his handsome son, patted William's back. "I'm sorry your mother isn't alive to see this day, laddie." Will nodded but said nothing. He was too happy and relieved that the ceremony was over to entertain even one sad thought.

"You're the loveliest bride that ever was, my girl," William overheard Helen's father, on his best behavior, whisper in her ear, and then her father turned to Will: "Lucky lad, you are!"

"Ach! No rain on your weddin' day — that means you won't have many children, aye!" Helen's brother, also named William but known as Davey, teased her.

Jamie Barrie had come to the wedding with his older, spinster sister, Jane Ann, who was his invalid mother's main caregiver. William noticed that the two left shortly after the ceremony, Jamie looking particularly hunched-over and glum. But William was too elated to give Jamie's dark mood deep thought. He knew Jamie would be returning to university in Edinburgh on the next train, in order that Helen and Will could have his attic bedroom in Strath View as their "honeymoon suite," until Will had to leave for Natal. *Perhaps Jamie is having regrets about sharing his bed?* Will thought briefly, then turned his attention back to his radiant bride.

When Helen had approached William some months before their wedding with the idea of emigrating, at first he'd strongly resisted. He loved his job at the Kirrie railway station, where he felt appreciated, valued. He was the person anxious travelers relied on. He was the one the town's merchants and the factory bosses trusted with their costly freight. He went so far as to memorize the current train schedules. He knew the railway's telegraphic code book by heart, even the alphabetic code invented by the American Samuel Morse, which, with its rhythmic clicks, sounded to Will like music.

In Kirriemuir, William had justifiably gained a reputation for being a solid, bright dependable, young man — a rarity anywhere, in any age. He was, they all thought, the ideal railway station clerk.

For Will, his work also took on an element of art, even poetry. When he looked out at the lines of train tracks facing the small, stone, gable-roofed station building, he saw life-metaphors: *We humans are all like railway cars,* he thought, *only on different, sometimes parallel, sometimes merging or diverging tracks.* He was especially enamored of the steam locomotives' engines — their bulk and power, their hiss and screech and rumble, their strong arms pushing their wheels ever forward. He even loved the sight and smell of the smoke plumes they left in their wake. He would often sketch these engines in his spare time — their tubular, black bodies; flat, round faces; and porkpie-hat-like smoke stacks.

Though in a quick, simple sketch these engines might appear cartoonish, even comical, William knew their strength was formidable. He'd count the cars each engine could pull and calculate the weight of their cargo, then think: *No other man-made form of land transportation could do what a train can do. The railway and the telegraph — what remarkable new human inventions. What a historic time to be alive!*

Everything about trains had fascinated William Black since he was a small boy. Kirriemuir's original train station had opened in 1854, the same year that the Great North of Scotland Railway opened, six years before Will was born. But the stationhouse where he now worked was completed in 1871, and he'd closely followed its construction as a ten-year-old. In fact, he'd spent a good part of his youth watching the trains come and go from his solitary perch on the Commonty.

Will often recalled his first train ride — the gentle rocking back and forth of the car, the slow-but-steady, chugging-bucking, forward motion on the narrow-gauge tracks. It was just like riding a horse, he thought, but this horse was immense, man-made, coal-fed, and belched steam and sooty, acrid smoke. It huffed and puffed, hooted and clanked and clomped. Outside, bystanders waved in amazement as it passed. Will raised his window to wave back. He could feel himself falling in love.

To finally work as a clerk at the Kirriemuir station after he'd finished his secondary schooling was for him a dream come true.

But Helen, his other true love, was persuasive. She knew Will well enough to know what would likely change his mind. She showed him one of the newspaper ads that Jamie Barrie had clipped and mailed to her from Edinburgh: There were openings for "experienced railway men" in Natal, South Africa. It would be a "golden opportunity" for the "right young men" to advance their prospects in "the expanding colonies." *There will be sunshine,* Helen stressed, *no more of this dampness and chill... And trains, Will—new trains—more trains! You'll still be working with trains!*

To make Helen happy, Will agreed to apply. And when he received a prompt acceptance, Helen's enthusiasm infected him too. The general manager of the company, Natal Government Railways, a fellow-Scotsman named David Hunter, wrote from Durban that Will was just the sort of "skilled and educated fellow" he was looking for.

Hunter's lofty letter praised the Natal Government

Railway as "the most efficient form of transport" in South Africa, "providing improved speed and carrying capacity and serving to extend frontiers and accelerate development" within the region. Hunter said Will would likely be placed on the North Coast line, at a station about eight miles north of Durban, called Avoca, which had only been open since May, 1878. "Unlike the South Coast line, which hugs the coastline," Hunter's letter went on, "this railway is located inland, with the gradient problems linked to the undulating terrain." The small town of Avoca, he said, was situated on a vast sugar estate called Rose Hill.

Hunter closed his letter by telling Will he wanted him to start work for them right away. Will would have to leave for Durban in Scotland's winter — South Africa's summer. *If all went well, Hunter stressed, Will's wife, Helen, could come out and join him in Natal as soon as conceivably possible.*

"All will go well! *It will,* my Will!" ebullient Helen insisted, dancing a quick jig. "You will light the way. I will follow soon! ... Oh! Rose Hill!" she sang, "Oh, my love is like a red, red rose!"

Helen's unquestioned confidence and excitement buoyed Will, but his mind still reeled. This was not just a day trip on Kirrie's railway to Edinburgh, which was the farthest he'd ever been from home. No, Natal was more than six thousand miles away, and the sea voyage took weeks. He'd never been out to sea for any length of time, and the few times he'd gone fishing off Scotland's coast, in a small boat mercilessly tossed by winds and rain, he'd gotten seasick. His friends called him a "landlubber."

His thoughts ricocheted. Hadn't he read harrowing accounts of shipwrecks? Oh, but those widely publicized narratives of the dangers of sea travel mostly dated to the age of sailing ships, he recalled. Now, in the modern age of steamships, he realized, shipwrecks were probably a thing of the past. Steamships were as strong and as sure as steam locomotives! Yes, he could certainly trust a modern steamship to deliver him to firm, dry land soon enough.

Of course he wouldn't be the first Scotsman to dare such a wild adventure. No, millions of other Scots had poured out of their homeland across vast oceans in search of greater success in far-off lands. *If others could do it,* Will told himself, *why then so can I!*

Plus, Africa was no longer considered "the white man's graveyard," as people used to say. No, thanks to the new drug developed by French chemists, called quinine, the number-one threat, malaria, was not as life threatening as it used to be. In fact, one of Will's heroes, the Scottish medical missionary-explorer David Livingstone, had been the first person to use quinine in Africa, and he credited it with keeping him alive.

Will also recalled reading about Livingstone's enjoyment of his life in Africa: "The mere animal pleasure of traveling in a wild unexplored country is very great," Livingstone wrote. "Great exercise imparts elasticity to the muscles, fresh and healthy blood circulates through the brain, the mind works well, the eye is clear, the step is firm." Before long, William was as convinced as Helen that Natal, South Africa, beckoned them both.

In the weeks between their wedding day and the day Will left Kirriemuir by train for the port, the newlyweds got little sleep.

They had loved each other all their young lives; they'd been childhood sweethearts. As teenagers they had stolen kisses and fully clothed embraces whenever they had the chance. But when Helen had pressed Will for more, he told her it was "bad luck" to break God's rules, they must wait to be "properly married." So after that long-anticipated, life-altering day in late-October, they spent every night of their newly married lives together making love through the night.

Will had long known the fragrance of Helen's hair when he'd wrapped his arm around her shoulder, the softness of the skin on her neck whenever he kissed her there, the strength of her tapered fingers when they walked hand in hand, the sight of her bare feet running on the green commonty on a warm and sunny summer afternoon. But now that they were husband-and-wife, sharing one bed, naked beneath warm quilts on these late-autumn nights, Will could explore all of her, trace every smooth curve of her body, taste every inch of her skin. Every night, then, in Jamie Barrie's attic bedroom at Strath View, Will became a man on a mission — to please his beloved, one-and-only Helen. And when their bodies joined, when they became one, he felt his life was complete.

The townspeople remarked among themselves how marriage had changed the spirited Helen David. Some said she'd become "subdued." Others used the word "serene." A few claimed that William Black had managed to "tame" her.

"And it's about time, too!" one old biddy clucked.

It was true that Helen's demeanor had changed since her wedding in late October. At first, in the weeks before William left for Natal, she carried herself as if in a daze. Nights filled with newly discovered lovemaking and little sleep had put her in an altered state, as if she were drunk, though she hadn't touched a drop. In fact, Helen never drank—out of a deep-seated fear that one day she might learn to like whiskey as much as her father did.

Helen smiled benignly at everyone she passed along Kirriemuir's narrow winding streets and wider roads; she hummed softly to herself at the linen factory, instead of singing aloud as before; and she stopped stepping away from her place in the work line to dance a little jig.

Helen's co-workers were grateful for the change that had come over her. She no longer broke the rules and brought the foreman's wrath upon them all. She was a married woman now, a lofty status they all aspired to. Marriage had made her more mature and more obedient (they presumed). Their hearts softened somewhat toward her. They smiled back at her, almost approvingly. They were also glad to know she would soon be leaving for the colonies, perhaps (they hoped) never to return.

Then the day came in early December for William to leave Kirriemuir to begin his long journey to the eastern coast of South Africa. The couple agreed that Helen would bid him farewell at the Kirrie railway station, along with all the others who had come to say good-bye. The platform was crowded with the young man's local admirers, well-wishers, neighbors, and friends. A light snow was beginning to fall, and people pulled their capes and shawls tighter around their shoulders and huddled together as they all waited for Will's train to depart.

Finally, the time came. William embraced Helen, leaning his face into her hair and inhaling her fragrance deeply, as if for strength. William's father, John Black, dressed in a black suit and coat as though attending a funeral, approached his son stiffly with an extended right hand. "This is for you, laddie," he said, pressing his own cherished gold-plated pocket watch into Will's hands, "now it is your time."

William thanked his father in a quick embrace, tucked the pocket watch into his vest pocket, then reached for his large suitcase, waved bravely to the crowd like a soldier going off to war, and boarded the train.

Early that morning, as they'd packed to leave their "honeymoon suite," Jamie Barrie's attic bedroom-study at Strath View — William for his overseas journey to their new life in Natal and Helen to return, temporarily, to her parents' cottage in Southmuir — Helen ran her fingers along the spines of the leather-bound books in Jamie's bookcase. Prior to spending the past six weeks here at Strath View, she had never seen so many beautiful books in one, private bedroom, especially books belonging to and beloved by one sole person. The Barries had always emphasized book learning and higher education, she knew, but Helen had never before seen Jamie's own book collection. There was Shakespeare, of course, and so many others — among them, Wordsworth and Spencer and Fennimore Cooper; Hume and Bacon and Adam Smith; and Scotland's favorite sons, Carlyle, Scott and Burns.

In the small cottage in which Helen had grown up, there had never been room for books, only room enough for life's essentials, cooking, eating, sleeping, and working at the loom. There were no bookcases, no writing desk, like Jamie's here beside his bed. The leather spines of Jamie's books felt smooth as skin against Helen's fingertips. She wished she could stay in this quiet, book-lined room and read them, one by one, while she waited for word that she could leave Kirriemuir to join Will in Natal. These books would fill the long hours of waiting and take her away from the reality of their forced separation.

Then it was time to present Will with a surprise, a book she'd known he'd wanted for a long time, the English artist and art critic John Ruskin's *Elements of Drawing,* published in 1857, and hugely popular among aspiring artists. Will opened the paper wrapping slowly, savoring the suspense, and when he saw what the gift was, he danced Helen around Jamie's room. He promised her he'd spend every spare moment during the time they'd be apart busily studying and practicing his art.

While helping Will pack his suitcase, Helen tucked into one side another gift, meant to be a surprise for him later — a long, thin, tin, watercolor paint box, along with several paint brushes and pencils, a book-size artist's pad, and a pad of writing paper. Ruskin's book, she'd been told, also taught watercolor painting, and she was sure Will would enjoy learning how.

She had saved her factory wages to buy these gifts at W.B. Mills Printer and Publisher in the town square, the shop where Jamie Barrie had long bought many of his books, the place, in fact, where he as a child had seen his first puppet show. The owner, forty-five-year-old William Mills himself, had explained to Helen the glories of watercolor painting.

"We've come a long way," he lectured her, "since the Egyptians made watercolor paints out of ground stone, insect blood, and fruit juices and painted on papyrus! Now anyone can paint anywhere, anytime, on white paper, with these wondrous little cakes of water-soluble colors nestled in this handy, portable metal case. It's affordable, too — not like the wooden paint box over here."

Helen gazed longingly at the wooden box, which looked to her like a miniature writing desk, with its smooth, varnished surface, large hinged lid, and pullout drawers filled with rows of colorful cakes of watercolor paint and long, slender, camel-hair brushes.

Mr. Mills, though, knowing Helen and her family were people of modest means, stressed the advantages of the other, less-pricey gift. He tapped on its tin lid. "This Prang paint set is manufactured in America — look," he said, pointing to the label and redirecting Helen's gaze. "Made by the American Crayon Company, and sold all over the world to students of art." He opened the lid. "See, there are eight pans of water-color paint — cadmium yellow, Prussian blue, viridian green, violet, carmine red, raw sienna, burnt umber, and sepia. William will be able to mix these to create whatever colors he needs."

Mills looked admiringly at Helen — the honey color of her hair, the blue-green of her eyes, the rose of her cheeks. *Someone should paint her portrait in oils,* he thought, *while she is still so young and beautiful.*

"Yes, I'm sure your William would much prefer this one!" Mills continued, wishing he were twenty years younger, wishing, just for a fleeting second, that he were the lucky William Black. "He'll be able to carry it with him everywhere he goes and paint whatever he sees. Why, when you two come back to Kirrie in a few years, no doubt William will be a good enough artist to join the new Scottish Society of Water-Colour Painters!"

As the train bearing Will pulled slowly away from the station, Helen tried to imagine his surprise when he came to open her second gift. *When would that be? And where? What would he say? And think?*

Suddenly, as the train began to vanish, becoming smaller and smaller, like a toy, then turning the bend, the reality of his leaving struck her like an archer's arrow. No, she thought, she needed to see his face when he opened his gift! She needed to feel his grateful embrace! She needed to be with him! They belonged together! Why was he leaving her? No! Stop! Come back!

She began to run along the slippery, snow-flecked platform after the train, holding her hat and dodging the dispersing crowd. She felt dizzy. She lost her footing and nearly fell. Neighbors helped her to a bench, brushed the snow from its seat, and let her sit down. They chattered and chirped around her like squirrels, trying to comfort and soothe her.

"Oh, you'll be seein' his pretty face again soon enou', lass!" one said.

"He's jus' pavin' the way for ye!" another chimed in.

"Good thing God a'mighty created the penny postage stamp," another intoned.

Helen returned to her parents' cottage that night as planned because Jamie Barrie was due to return from Edinburgh University on his winter recess the next day. Helen's mother Agnes saw that her daughter was unwell; she was feverish and bleeding heavily. Agnes, suspecting a miscarriage, put Helen to bed straightaway, where she remained for over two weeks.

Southmuir, Winter 1881-'82

As the winter solstice approached, with its shorter, colder days and longer, bitter nights, Helen ached for Will. Returning to her childhood bed, being cared for by her mother and spoon-fed barley soup as if she were still a child, these were backward steps for Helen, now a married woman. She wanted to be going forward. She wanted to be on the ship headed for sunny-warm Durban with her husband. She berated herself, *Why did we agree that he would go first, alone? I belong with him!*

At times, her spirit rebelled and her emotions swirled. She questioned their mutual decisions and her own impetuousness. People had often criticized her stubbornness and "bull-headedness," sometimes even to her face. "Helen David, why can't you be more docile, like the other girls?" one grade-school teacher had complained. But Helen couldn't help but be who she was, could she? *Was it possible to be someone other than who you were meant to be?* Her thoughts flew in circles until she fell back into a deep sleep, while her mother wiped her fiery forehead with a cool, dry cloth.

Jamie Barrie came to visit as soon as he could. He sat beside Helen's sickbed and told her silly stories, playing the same role he always played with his invalid mother Margaret Ogilvy, believing that storytelling was the best medicine.

"Early this morning," he began, dramatically gesturing and enacting each phrase, "I opened my window, awakened by the shivering of a starving sparrow against the frosted glass. As the snowy sash creaked in my hand, he made off to the waterspout that suspends its tangles of ice over a gaping tank, and, rebounding from that, with a quiver of his little black breast, bobbed through the network of wire and joined a few of his fellows in a forlorn hop round the henhouse in search of food. ..."

Helen watched her dear friend and listened intently as his story unfolded. When he finished, she said only, "I wish I were a bird. I wish I could fly to Will."

"Ah. Fly," Jamie said, thoughtfully. "Yes... I often dream of that... If only we humans could fly!"

By Christmas week Helen was well enough to return to work, but this time her co-workers were concerned. Helen's face had lost its high color, her eyes were ringed in dark circles, and she seemed too thin for her tall, slim frame. She didn't sing, or even hum, anymore. She didn't break the factory's rules by dancing. She didn't smile.

They talked among themselves: What might they do to get their old, high-spirited Helen back?

"Aye, there's only one solution to that," one of them said. "Bring William back!"

On Christmas day Agnes prepared a special dinner for her family, hoping it might improve Helen's flagging appetite and knowing this would likely be the last Christmas Helen would spend at home for some time. Earlier in the week, Helen's father Sandy and her brother Davey had gone hunting together, as they often did, this time bagging a wild goose, which Agnes dressed and cooked for Christmas dinner. She served it with a stuffing made of apples, oats, and herbs, plus bowls of boiled potatoes and parsnips.

Helen sat silently at her place at the table, pushing her food delicately from place to place on her plate but lifting little to her mouth, listening and remembering. She remembered when her father had taken her hunting, too, when she was younger and how he'd praised her marksmanship. Once, she'd shot a hare on the run, and another time, a pheasant in full flight. "That's my girl," her father had hooted, slapping his thigh. "Nobody'll ever cross *you*, my lass!"

Helen listened to her mother talk of Christmas, as she had every year, as a "pagan holiday, picked up by the Catholics." Agnes pronounced it "Christ's Mass," adding: "*We* go to church services. Those Catholics go to a thing called *mass*, where they mass together and let the pope tell 'em what to do. If the pope says, 'Go out and cut down a fir tree and put it in yer house,' they'll do it 'cause the pope says so."

"The Barries aren't Catholics, and they have a Christmas tree in their parlor decorated with ornaments and real candles," Davey said. "And Queen Victoria's not Catholic, and she puts up a Christmas tree at her castle in Balmoral every year."

"Well, we're not the Barries, are we — and I'm not Queen Victoria livin' in a castle!" Agnes shot back. "Trees belong outside, not inside the house! Any fool knows that. Besides, where would we put one in here? On my loom? Wi' the candle wax drippin' all over my weavin'? Aye, worshippin' trees in the house is a pagan practice, and I'm ag'in' it!"

"And we already know you're against Christmas gift-giving too," Davey said flatly. "Maybe old Charles Dickens had the Scots in mind when he created that miserly character Ebenezer Scrooge."

"Miserly, eh?" Agnes sputtered. "Who takes care a' you? Who puts food on the table?"

"*I* shot this goose," Davey said, pointing to his plate.

Sandy David jumped in to change the subject and save the day. "Hogmanay is the holiday for me!" he announced jovially, as if this were news to the family. Everyone in Kirriemuir knew to expect Sandy at their doorstep soon after the stroke of midnight on New Year's Eve, bearing a small gift of oatcakes Agnes had made and hoping he'd be the first tall, handsome man to cross their threshold, thereby bringing them good luck in the year ahead. He considered this one of his life's missions. Oh, yes, and of course he'd stay for a "wee dram," before moving on to the next neighbor's cottage. Then, when he'd exhausted them all, he would stagger home, just before the sun decided to rise on New Year's Day.

Helen had lost her appetite for food. She barely had the strength to pick up her fork. Her hands and feet felt colder than ever, and the metal fork felt too cold in her hand. She couldn't remember a winter when she'd felt so cold.

She looked out the low, square window beside her mother's loom and saw a group of laughing children dressed warmly in woolen caps, scarves and mittens, carrying their shiny new Christmas skates and heading for the Den, where the ground, as every winter, had been flooded and converted to a smooth, frozen skating pond. Helen didn't envy these children. She had been young once, and she had had enough of the cold. Now, at nineteen, she was a married woman who would soon be joining her handsome husband in ever-sunny, ever-warm South Africa.

During the first weeks that stretched into months in early 1882, Helen lived on love letters. Florid letters filled with brotherly love arrived from Jamie Barrie, now only months away from earning his degree from Edinburgh University. And long, romantic letters at last reached her from Natal.

Jamie wrote of the "grind, grind, grind" of his studies, the hours he spent "toiling in the University

Library." He wrote of his loneliness and how much he missed "marching away into the glens" in Kirriemuir with her. He confided in her, as ever, something he feared he could not tell his mother or sisters: He'd been experiencing bouts of "the blackest depression" and terrible headaches. "Write soon!" he begged her. "Your letters make me dance and sing — though not as well as you — alone in my lodgings."

But it was Will's first letter from Durban, which reached Kirriemuir in late-January, that brought renewed life to the ailing Helen. The letter was several pages long, scripted in William's neat, uniform hand. Helen studied his handwriting as if she'd never seen anything quite so exquisite. She could tell he must have taken pains to make each line of words, written in blue ink, a work of art; all of the words had the same forward tilt, like ocean waves; all of the ascending and descending characters were precisely the same height and depth; and the breaths between the lines of blue-wave words looked to her like sighs. Because they had never before been apart for any length of time, this was the first letter from William that Helen had ever received.

The folded pages enclosed a small watercolor painting, the size of a postal card, inscribed on the back, "1st watercolour drawing — Harbour Bay, Durban — Christmas, 1881." Anxious to read Will's letter, Helen only glanced at the painting. She could see it had been painted hurriedly. There was a large body of water in the foreground and a big sky over all, both executed in the same pale, watery blue; there were small boats with thin dark masts bobbing in the harbor, clumps of trees dotting the shoreline, and — what was that in the background? — cliffs?

It was indeed a childlike effort, the sort of painting only a mother would dare display. Its best feature, Helen thought, was that it was bright. Even the pale blue sky seemed infused with warmth and light. Yes, she had to concede, William's first watercolor painting was a picture of hope.

Helen propped the small painting up as if on an easel in front of her as she sat by the warmth of the hearth, and, heart pounding, began to read to herself.

My darling Hellion,

Now that I am on solid ground again, I can post this to you to let you know that I, as vanguard, have arrived at our destination — and safely. I hope that this letter finds you well and that you had a happy Christmas with the family.

The sea voyage was long, monochromatic (blue and more blue!), but not unpleasant. The weather conditions were favourable, for the most part. Thanks to the great seaworthiness of the vessel — modern ocean liners do not bounce about on the high seas the way sailboats and fishing boats do, I'm pleased to report! — I was not seasick too often. Steamships are sturdy, strong, and speedy, like steam locomotives — only these ships leave tracks behind them instead of following them full-steam-ahead.

Beyond a cordial "good day," I did not mingle much with the other passengers, most of whom were young, emigrating families who liked to keep to themselves; nor did I talk with single ladies, nor play cards with the bachelors. I did, however, tour every part of the ship that I could, to see and try to understand it all, even the chain lockers and the engine room and the rudder assembly. I also became friends with the bo'sun, who liked to explain the inner workings and tell tall tales of shipboard life and past experiences.

But my greatest companion on the voyage was John Ruskin, in book form, many thanks to you, my darling. "Uncle John Ruskin" (as he will hereinafter be known to us, since I feel his book, written as three letters—each beginning with "My dear Reader," and closing with "Very faithfully yours, J. Ruskin"—as well as all of the choice bits of wisdom in it, were written especially for and to me) and I spent many instructive hours together. What I've learned, most of all so far, is how much I still need to learn about drawing and painting!

Ah, painting! Did I mention to you that I now have a paint box of my very own? It seems that an angel delivered it to me while my back was turned. Indeed, it was Heaven-sent. I've been looking for that angel to thank her appropriately, but she is nowhere to be seen. You can be assured that when I do find her I will shower her with kisses!

You will see from the enclosed that I have already begun to paint this new world. But perhaps the less said about this painting the better. Suffice it to say that it proves I am a poor student, already ignoring Uncle John's teachings. He preaches patience, tenderness, and, above all, <u>care</u>. He says, "If you have not time to draw ... carefully, do not draw at all—you are merely wasting your work and spoiling your taste."

Nevertheless, I was anxious to try, at least, to show you my first impressions of Durban, before even stepping foot on Africa's soil. (Our ship had to wait in the harbour for the tide to change before we could disembark.)

And, on the subject of soil, I had attempted some of the exercises in Ruskin's book while still out at sea. One of the first, though, calls for a stone. "Go out into your garden, or into the road," our Uncle John says, "and pick up the first round or oval stone you can find" because "if you can draw that stone, you can draw anything." Well, I was stopped short right there, not having a handy garden nor any available roads on the ship!

So, my darling, at that point in my lessons, my thoughts turned to you there in our dear old Kirrie, with its unlimited supply of ancient stones. And I thought, if anyone can help me win this battle with the pencil and paintbrush, it's my very own Hellion. Would you, therefore, go hunting for the perfect, smooth, oval stone from home —just small enough to fit comfortably in the palm of your hand—to bring to me here when you come to join me? With that magic stone, conveyed in your beautiful hand, I'm sure my latent artistic talents are sure to come alive and I shall be able to "draw anything"!

I have, of course, only just arrived and have barely regained my land-legs. But I can say that my first impres-

sions of this new world are all positive. Heaven itself could
not be more balmy and embracing! I look forward to ex-
ploring and observing this port city and its surrounds in the
days ahead and sharing with you my discoveries — in both
simple words and amateurish watercolour pictures. Soon,
too, I will meet my new employers and begin my real work
here. The act of drawing and painting pleases the child
inside, but railway work is for men.

> *I love you, my darling, and miss you terribly already.*
> *Please give my regards to the family.*
> *My deepest love to you forever,*
>
> *Yours faithfully, William*

The task that Will had set for Helen became her highest
mission. One mild Sunday afternoon that winter, when
Jamie was home in Kirrie on a brief visit to see his ailing
mother, Helen enlisted Jamie's help in hunting for the
perfect smooth, oval stone. Knowing that long walks
were one of Jamie's favorite pastimes when he wasn't
closeted, monklike, writing and studying, she was certain he would be a more than willing partner.

As they walked together, Helen focusing on the
stony shoulder of the road and Jamie dreamily gazing
skyward, he lectured Helen on the geology of the area,
which he'd learned in a recent course at university,
where they'd used the textbook *Principles of Geology,*
by Charles Lyell.

"Lyell was from Kirrie, you know," Jamie said.

"Not *here*," Helen said, doubtfully.

"Well, near enough. He was born just up the road in Kinnordy, about eighty-five years ago." Jamie paused to hear her reaction, but Helen was stooping to pick up another stone. "Yes, old Kirrie is a rather remarkable town. Scores and scores of houses in it have sent their sons to college — and by what a struggle! — some to make their way to the front in their professions. Lyell was one of them. But his family didn't have to struggle. They were prosperous landowners."

Helen examined and discarded stone after stone: not smooth enough, not small enough, not comfortable enough in her hand... She turned to Jamie absently, "And his book?"

"His central argument, as I recall," Jamie said, leaning on his walking stick as Helen stopped to inspect more stones, "was that the present is the key to the past, which is like what David Hume said, 'all inferences from experience suppose ... that the future will resemble the past.' Geologically speaking, this meant to Lyell that remains from the distant past can and should be explained by reference to geological processes now in operation, which are directly observable. He drew all the explanations in his book from his own field studies, many conducted right around here."

Helen nodded in Jamie's direction, then returned to closely studying a particular stone. "Well, we're doing field studies right here and now, aren't we? Observe this!" She cupped the stone in one hand. It was a small, smooth, oval stone, coal-gray, with tiny white speckles in it like stars in the night sky. "This one feels right to me. What do you think?"

"I think it's a wee piece of granite with flecks of silvery silica through it, which has been naturally rounded by thousands of years of tumbling and stumbling along the bottom of a prehistoric river."

"I think it's my lucky stone, the one I'll hold tight to and hand-deliver to Will in Durban."

"I have heard," Jamie added, "that the old drovers carried small stones like this one as charms to ward off evil spirits."

"All the better!" Helen said, kissing the plump little stone, and then, with restored exuberance, kissing her friend's cheek.

Between late-January and early-March 1882, Helen and William's letters crisscrossed the ocean, borne by the reliable Union Line, the steamship company awarded the British government contract to carry mail to South Africa. One ship took six weeks to make the round trip from Southampton to Durban, and a different ship set off once a week. So, if all went well, Helen could expect a letter from Will every week, and she in turn would send one off to him.

Helen was careful to hide her excitement in front of Lizzie, the postmistress at the post office in Kirriemuir's town square, who fancied herself a veritable town crier of everyone's news. Some townsfolk claimed Lizzie went so far as to steam letters open to read them herself, before the recipients did. How else, people wondered, did so much private information and gossip get out and about all over town?

"And how is our William doin' out there in the colonies?" old Lizzie inquired shyly, as if she didn't know.

"He's doing well, thank you," Helen answered coolly, but her hands trembled with anticipation as she accepted Will's latest letter and then posted her own to him.

The truth was that Helen lived for Will's letters. They fed her, strengthened her, and buoyed her. They made her look forward and kept her from sinking back into the despondency she'd felt after his departure. She'd begun to enjoy her mother's cooking again and hum her favorite tunes at work. She walked tall, as if fully inflated by hope, and she smiled politely at people she passed on the street, all the while counting the days before she could say good-bye to all of them.

Each of Will's letters contained a surprise, such as a pressed, pink bougainvillea flower, or a pinch of rich soil, or a pencil sketch or small painting he'd made of things he knew she would want to see: grassy landscapes, scrubby trees, beehive-shaped thatched Zulu huts set in a circular *kraal,* chubby African babies with smiling eyes. His earliest watercolor paintings, though not fine art, she knew, told stories she could understand: Will was happy there. And his happiness infected her.

"You will love it here, my darling Hellion," he wrote. "The sky is your favourite shade of blue, and the weather is so sunny and warm you will only need to wear light cotton frocks. You can leave all your heavy woollies back home in Kirrie!"

In another letter William quoted a missionary, the Rev. Lewis Grout, who said, 'So far as I can judge, the British crown lays claim to no dependency of more promise as a field for emigration that the colony of Natal.'

The people, Will wrote, "are friendly, for the most part, especially the Africans I've met so far, who seem to be particularly guileless." Will related a story he'd heard about an American missionary who'd been alarmed, on his arrival in Natal, at the sight of semi-naked Zulu men armed with spears. This young missionary, named Tyler, asked his mentor, a Rev. Lindley, 'Is it safe to dwell among this people?' To which Lindley responded, 'Brother Tyler, you are safer here than in the streets of Boston.'

"The exceptions, though," Will wrote, "are some of the Boers who resent the British 'invasion,' as they call it. They can get downright mean about it, especially when they're liquored up, and they like to get liquored up, I'm told. But I keep my distance. I choose to go out alone into the countryside, rather than visit the city's saloons. 'Trouble' is not what I'm looking for!"

William never wrote of politics or economics because he was too young and new there to step back and objectively view the world he was immersing himself in. He knew that South Africa's railway networks were being built "at breakneck speed," as one official put it, to carry the wealth of goods produced and mined within the country to the waiting ships at port. The excitement surrounding this rapid industrialization made William feel that he was part of something big and vibrant and that his future with the Natal Government Railways was bright.

He was aware, of course, of the tensions between the British and Boers and the various bloody battles each had had with the indigenous tribes in recent years. The vivid memories of the brutal Anglo-Zulu War of 1879 were fresh in everyone's minds. But Will didn't take sides; and besides, that was the past. He was not a military man, dressed to the nines in a tight-fitting bright red jacket and white pith helmet, glorying in war stories. No, he was a new, proud employee of the Natal Government Railways, and his focus was forward.

The letter from Will that Helen most enjoyed rereading was the one that contained the pinch of Africa's soil:

… I've been made a stationmaster! Now, Hellion, you'll have to call me your Lord and Master! The station is Avoca — as Mr. Hunter had mentioned in his letter — and it is only eight miles north of Durban on the coast. It is still remote, with no village to speak of, just a sugar mill and a hotel and the Avoca Hall, where the Freemasons have their meetings, Sunday services are held, and, they tell me, occasional concerts are given by the widely scattered inhabitants. There are two sugar plantations in the vicinity.

The cottage I've found for us is less than an hour's walk from the station. It needs work, but I know between the two of us, we can make it a home. We can raise chickens, and ducks, and maybe goats; and you can have a kitchen garden, planting pumpkin, sweet potatoes, and maize, like the Africans do. The soil is so rich and fertile! I will enclose a pinch of it in this envelope for you to touch...

William closed each letter with outpourings of love. "I miss you, Hel. The birds here are singing for you, calling your name, as am I." Sometimes he even added snippets of a Robbie Burns love poem, such as the one Helen had sung to him in Kirrie, but this time preserving Burns' "lass":

> So fair art thou, my bonny lass,
> So deep in love am I;
> And I will love thee still, my dear,
> Till a' the seas gang dry.

Edinburgh, February 1882

After his brief visit to Kirriemuir and his walk with Helen to hunt for her lucky stone, the thought finally crystalized in Jamie Barrie's mind as he rode the train back to Edinburgh to resume his university studies: *Helen would soon be gone! Gone!*

As the train jolted along, so did his thoughts: His dear friend would be leaving Scotland to live in the colonies — *and this had been his idea!* He had pushed the first domino that sent the rest falling inevitably forward. His heart suddenly ached. He felt struck, as if by cannon fire, with worry and remorse. *And he only had himself to blame.*

He watched the cold winter rain pelt the window of the train, blurring the view of Scotland's southern undulating countryside. Or was it tears blurring his eyes? He listened to the loud chugging of the train. Or was it the thudding of his heart?

One of the first tasks he set for himself after returning to university was to do research in the Upper Library. He needed to know more about the place where Helen was heading. He already knew some things about

Britain's colonization of South Africa, of course, but not enough, he felt. He knew, for example, that South Africa's history—especially since the British swaggered in—was bellicose and bloody. But since the science of warfare had never been of any interest to him whatsoever, Jamie had paid scant attention to the headlines.

But now that "his" Helen, his best childhood friend, his confidante, was about to actually leave their hometown and everyone in it, and voyage to Africa— *Africa! on her own!*—he was anxious to learn all that he could. Knowledge is power, he knew. Armed with more knowledge, perhaps, he might have the power to dissuade her. *Perhaps,* he thought, *it isn't too late for Helen to change her mind. Perhaps she, then, could convince William to return to Kirrie soon too. And then all would be well again, surely.*

With the aid of a kindly librarian, Jamie combed through the new, handwritten, alphabetical card catalogue to unearth books and articles on South Africa's recent history. He read in thick files, filled with fading newspaper clippings, about Britain's battles with the Boers in 1880 in the Transvaal, where the British military experienced disaster after disaster—at Bronkhorst Spruit, Laing's Nek, Ingogo and finally and worst of all, at Majuba Hill. He learned that the results of these battles had been deeply humiliating to the world's mightiest imperial power.

Their attempts to test the individual freedom and skill-at-arms of the hardy Boer farmer, whose Dutch forefathers arrived in South Africa over two hundred years before, had ended in failure. To the unyielding Boers, whose marksmanship and talent for guerilla warfare was legendary, an enemy that crossed the open veld in scarlet uniforms and white sun helmets expecting to fight according to certain fixed rules was merely an easy target. To the proud British, their defeat was a blot on their honor.

Fresh, red, human blood, Jamie saw, never seemed to dry in South Africa, where war was endemic. The Boers fought with the Zulus, the British fought with the Boers, and the Zulus fought with the British. Just the year before the Anglo-Boer battles in 1880, there were the Zulu Wars, most notably the battle at Rorke's Drift, which had received the most press in Britain, Jamie discovered. After the British experienced a bloodbath at the hands of thousands of Zulu warriors armed with only assegais and cowhide shields at Isandhlwana, their victory at Rorke's Drift in Zululand provided much-needed positive publicity for the British government.

"The defense of Rorke's Drift was a triumph of skill, discipline, courage and stamina," one newspaper editorial read. But it was a small triumph. One hundred men, armed with Martini-Henry rifles, considered the best service rifle of all, and unlimited ammunition, held off for twelve hours "a magnificently brave horde" of several thousand Zulu warriors who were "effectively without firearms." However, the commentator wrote, "a centuries-old tradition laid down that this was the kind of thing that the British infantryman was expected to do."

Feeling sickened by these accounts of so much bloody war, Jamie sought earlier information about the region from the finest source available, the eighth edition of Scotland's pride, the Encyclopedia Britannica, published in 1858. He pulled out Volume XV and turned to page 802, where he began reading under the section headed "Natal." His eyes skimmed along, taking in the salient facts.

> This country was discovered by the Portuguese on Christmas-day 1498, and named Natal in honour of the day. They found it inhabited by a portion of the Kafir race, divided into small tribes, not unfrequently at war with one another, but kind and hospitable to strangers. ... Little more is known of it till 1810, when a remarkable man arose in the neighbouring country of the Zulu-Kafirs. This was Chaka.... The united tribes under his rule became a great nation, and conquered and destroyed other tribes of Kafirs far and wide. Nearly the whole population of Natal was swept away, being either annihilated or incorporated with the conquerors.

Jamie rubbed his eyes and shook his head. *Wars and more wars,* he thought. *So much blood. Why do men fight like this? Why do they feel such a need to annihilate or conquer each other?* But he felt compelled to continue reading the encyclopedia's fascinating account.

He learned that a small party of British emigrants settled in Natal in 1824, having been ceded a considerable part of the country by Chief Chaka himself. Thirteen years later, a party of Dutch Boers arrived in Natal from the Cape and was welcomed by the British settlers. But when they approached Chaka's successor to negotiate the acquisition of some land for themselves, they came to a bad end:

> ... so completely did the wily chief, by marks of friendship and hospitality, succeed in disarming the suspicion of his guests, that as they were on the point of leaving him, he induced them to present themselves without their fire-arms, before himself and an array of his most trusted warriors, whom he had ordered to be drawn up to do honour to them on their departure.
>
> The warriors chanted the war-song in honour of their guests. In a short time the chief himself intoned a song, in the course of which he uttered the terrible words "Kill the wizards!" In an instant the lines of savage warriors closed in on the sixty-six Boers, and butchered them to a man in cold blood. The chief then despatched a large force to attack the rest of the Boers, scattered in small encampments over the country. Some of them were surprised, and men, women, and children were murdered; others, who had time for defence, repulsed their assailants. A deadly war ensued between the Boers and the Zulus...

This is positively Shakespearean! Jamie thought. *"Kill the wizards!" — I must remember that line. ...* The drama of this surprisingly exciting encyclopedic narrative overruled his revulsion for war. He read on...

Of course, the Boers retaliated. One Sunday morning in 1838, with their wagons lashed together in a laager, or circular barricade, four hundred Boers fought off an attack of Zulu forces 12,000 strong:

> The Zulu warriors marched up in dense columns, and hour after hour strove in vain to storm the camp. Their close battalions were one after another shattered to pieces by the terrible fire of its defenders. At length, towards the afternoon, the Zulu army was observed to waver; then the Boers mounted their horses, opened their barricade, and charged their assailants, who broke and fled.

> The Boers pursued them for many a mile, shooting them down without mercy. The victors lost but two or three men, while the loss of the Zulus is said to have exceeded 2,000. After this the war continued with varied success...

Jamie closed his eyes to give his imagination full reign. On one side he saw thousands of Zulu warriors — tall, strong, nearly naked, their bodies shining like polished ebony, carrying long spears and man-size, handmade hide shields — defending to the death their territory and their way of life. On the other side he saw the ragtag army of fearless, burly Boers — with their long, unkempt beards and slouch hats, dressed in farm-work clothes, with belts of ammunition slung over their shoulders, gripping their old rifles for dear life — defending the farmland they'd claimed and the only way of life they ever knew.

And onto this tense, overrun stage Jamie saw white-helmeted, red-uniformed British soldiers ride in on their majestic horses — their handsome, aristocratic officers trained at Sandhurst or Woolwich or Norwich — to do the impossible: subdue the Zulus and govern the Boers, all the while spreading "civilization" and scientific advancement to these "lesser" peoples.

Jamie held his heavy head in his hands. What could he do? Should he warn Helen of the dangers she was about to sail into? He imagined her, his beloved leading lady — as tall and regal as a Zulu maiden and as fair-haired, steadfast and brave as a Boer wife, who herself belonged to a tribe that had fought bloody battles with the English for centuries — at the center of this stage, standing in the crossfire. Could her young husband protect her? Not likely. Jamie knew that William Black was no more a soldier than he himself was. Jamie's heart ached.

But he read on, looking for brighter spots in the Encyclopedia Britannica's story. In addition to its history, the four-and-a-half-page entry also spoke of Natal's natural beauty, its temperate climate, its geology, botany, educational programs, and religious divisions. It ended on the subject of agriculture, as if luring prospective emigrants:

Agriculture is steadily advancing. In the upper and cooler parts of the country the cultivation of wheat, oats, and other grains is rapidly increasing; the breeding of cattle and sheep is also making good progress. The manufacture of sugar is progressing very satisfactorily; several mills have been imported and are in operation; and at the beginning of 1856 it was considered that there were nearly 1,000 acres of cane under cultivation. There seems, too, no doubt that its production will be highly remunerative. Land is not a tenth of the price it brings in the West Indies and Mauritius, while labour is cheaper. Natal, moreover, has a great advantage over these islands in so far as a European can labour out of doors without danger to health.

Aye, Jamie thought, *the weather might well be favorable to one's health, but what about the whizzing bullets and spears?* He shivered at the thought. He must share this research with Helen. He must write a letter to her back in Kirriemuir today and warn her that's she's about to enter a lion's mouth.

He placed the encyclopedia volume back on the library shelf and, heavy hearted, walked back to his room across the quad, gripping his overcoat against the bitter wind. On the way, though, he thought of the explorers he so admired and even envied — like his intrepid friend Joseph Thomson — all those who had the physical strength and mental courage to venture into the unknown and brave the terrible risks. He only wished he could be like them.

Back in his small, book-lined garret, he sat at the wooden table he used as a desk and began writing a long letter to Helen, warning her of the dangers ahead and telling her what he'd learned from the encyclopedia. He tore it up, and began another, then another.

In the end, he mailed a short letter to her, wishing her well on her "great adventure" and telling her how strong and brave she was. He added, "Don't forget that lucky stone!" and signed the letter, "Yours aye, Jamie."

Leith, March 1882

Father and son Sandy and Davey David relished the chance to accompany Helen to Scotland's premier seaport at Leith without Agnes as chaperone. If either of them had had qualms about Helen's departure, neither let on. They were jovial company, talking with each other as Helen sat between them on the train journey from Kirriemuir to Leith, about their plans for the return train ride — where they'd stop off for "a wee dram" and to visit old friends and hunting mates. This was a special outing for them.

Davey, like Helen, had never been this far from Kirrie. He sat beside the window and remarked on the scenic views. It was a particularly clear day for early March, and the vista appeared endless.

At the port Sandy took command. He arranged for Helen's passage on the next small steamer that would take her to the ship at Southampton bound for Natal.

"Take care a' my girl here," Helen's father said to the uniformed man he assumed was in charge. "She's off to South Africa to join *her husband*," Sandy stressed, so the man would have no doubts about Helen's marital status.

The man looked Helen up and down, admiringly. "I'll be sure to keep an eye on her, aye," he said.

Helen, meanwhile, held a hankie to her nose to stanch the stench of fish, while her ears were bombarded by the seaport's raucous sounds. Clusters of seagulls squawked and circled overhead; fishmongers, pushing carts filled with fresh-caught white fish and herring, clattered along the cobblestone streets; fishwives, with large creels on their backs, dressed in brightly colored waistcoats and aprons, shouted their wares.

Davey stood beside his sister and admired the fine buildings surrounding the harbor, buildings owned by rich ship-owners and international merchants, he was sure. People richer than anyone in Kirriemuir.

When it was time for Helen to embark, Davey shook his sister's hand stiffly, in an effort to appear gallant, and wished her well. Sandy embraced his daughter and stroked her hair. With a choked voice, all he could manage to say was, "Good luck to ye, my lass." Helen showed her father the smooth good-luck stone resting in the palm of her right hand, and Sandy nodded approvingly.

On March 4, 1882, as if pulled by a force fiercer than the tides, Helen joyously joined the throngs that boarded the Union Line steamship at Southampton whose destination was Durban, to start her new life with her husband under Africa's skies. In her right hand she still held tightly to the smooth stone.

The first nights on board, though, Helen couldn't sleep. She found the slow rolling of the ship, the stifling air, and the loud nocturnal breathing of the other women in her steerage section disorienting. In the darkness she gripped the narrow sides of her bunk and questioned, *Where am I? What is happening? Who are these poor, unmoored strangers, and where are we all headed?* At first she longed for the old, solid, earthbound bed she'd left behind in Southmuir and the familiar sound of her sleeping parents' snoring that filled the night air of their small cottage. And then she reflected on her mother's good-bye, and in her sleeplessness she replayed their farewell scene.

Agnes was too ill, she'd said, to travel with Helen to Leith. Her bones, she'd said, and her joints, too, made it unbearably painful for her to walk any distance. No, she'd said, Helen should travel with her father and brother; they would look after her and see that she got off all right. Agnes's face, so clear in Helen's memory, was grotesquely puffed and her eyes swollen and red when she said farewell to her daughter. But she was also uncharacteristically stoic.

She didn't weep in front of Helen or whimper, *"What's t' become a' me?"* Instead, she surprised Helen with a gift — a soft, white linen shawl, hand-embroidered in dark blue thread in one corner with her maiden name, "Helen David of Kirriemuir." As she handed it to Helen she admonished, "Don't forget where ye come from, my girl!"

There is no sense looking backward, Helen told herself silently in the darkness of the ship's windowless and airless steerage section. She forced her mind to turn in the opposite direction, toward the future, to where this rolling behemoth of a steamship was headed, to South Africa, where her William was waiting for her. She thought of his smile, the smell of his hair and skin, the strength of his hands, his long, lean body wrapped around hers in bed. Soon she would never sleep alone again in her whole life. Soon they would have a home of their own. They would have a garden. They would start a family, a happy family of their very own.

These were the dreams that sustained her throughout the sea voyage, whether during the day, or asleep (or sleepless) in the night. And she fed these dreams, like adding logs to a hearth, with William's letters, which she read again and again, to the point of near-memorization. His words became lines to a play she enacted in her mind — a play in which, at least for the moment, she played both leading parts.

Natal, South Africa
18 January 1882
(My 21st birthday!)

My Darling Hellion,
    How I wish I could paint the sun's enveloping warmth, the birds' gleeful songs, and the heady fragrance of the countless flowers here. You will know for yourself soon enough, I trust, what a feast for the senses this region of the world is. Words and even drawings cannot adequately describe it. One must see and smell and taste and hear and feel the wonders of Africa for oneself. You'll see, my darling. Soon, soon!
    Until then, I am doing my best, in my bumbling beginner's fashion, to capture the beauty of everything around me in this new, colourful world with the water-colour paints you gave me. What an ideal gift, my Hellion! Only you would know how many hours of pleasure and companionship these paints give me as I wait not-so-patiently for you to join me out here on the other side of the world.
    I take my sketchpad everywhere I go now, along with the paint box. They fit easily into my knapsack, together with a bottle of water and sundry other necessities (a knife, a compass, a map, a hat, a handkerchief, an oat biscuit or two…) whenever I set out on what I like to call my "African adventures."
    These are adventures in <u>seeing</u> (which is not as easy as it seems!), though not to be confounded with big game

hunting. You know I could never kill an animal—especially the regal beasts of which Africa boasts. If I should happen upon one, though, on one of my solitary expeditions, I shall try to take a good look, then sketch him in my book quickly, just as soon as I've taken cover!

This is what I do on my free days: I set out on foot in a new direction and then after some time and distance, I allow a certain section of the landscape to stop me in my tracks. I then try to find a shaded spot beneath a scrubby tree where no one is likely to notice me, and I begin to sketch and paint. Believe me, Hellion, my efforts are rough in the extreme! Despite "Uncle John" Ruskin's lessons, my artistic talents have not advanced much since I sketched in my lesson book the view from our schoolhouse window instead of listening to the lessons. That schoolboy behaviour brought a sudden smack on the back of my head to success- fully discourage me. But now I am free of all that. There is no one here to judge or criticize me or my early efforts at artwork. Not even "Uncle John."

So I sit and I look out, and I ask myself, "Well, now, William lad, what do you <u>see</u>?" Indeed, I see that God him- self was the first artist, and we aspiring artists are nothing more than weak and minuscule imitators. I also see that God used all of the best and brightest colours in his paint box on this region of Africa. By the time he got to painting our wee town in Scotland, he had only dull sandstone reds and duller grays left.

For me, indeed, the act of painting has become an act of worship. The cliffs and hills, the verdant valleys, the overarching clear cerulean sky (when the rain clouds are not marching in; this is the rainy season) — these are my church now. Our Scottish churches lack colour, vibrancy, and warmth. Here, on this open, earthly plane, I praise God-the-Ultimate-Artist with every colourful, imitative brush stroke I make.

This is the magic of it: Although I am sitting still — except for the odd swatting of annoying flies or brushing away of equally annoying ants — I am transported. I am lifted out of my ordinary life and my usual way of seeing. I lose track of time. I forget what day it is. As I stare out at the distant horizon, I see it shimmering and I race (in place) to capture it. What colours to choose? What brush strokes to use? I dab and stab at the poor, unfortunate paper. I want to be good at this, but I know I am less than passable. Nevertheless, I am not letting that stop me! I march on!

One day this book of roughhewn watercolour paintings will help me to remember my first views of Africa while I awaited your longed-for arrival. And then, after you arrive, I will try to paint _you_, my darling — with the glinting sun in your hair and the gleam of new adventures in your eyes. When that day comes — and may God grant that day will come soon — I trust my painting skills will be worthy of your beauty. So I must keep practicing my painting, to be able to meet that day!

Your longing, loving husband,
William

Helen's closest bunkmates, some of whom were feeling seasick, others homesick, and all anxious about their futures, took a keen interest in Helen's collection of her husband's love letters and the strength she appeared to derive from them. They begged her to read one aloud to them one evening, almost as though it were a bedtime story. As they sat in a close circle looking up at Helen as if they were hungry birds, Helen chose this letter, in an effort to raise their hopes that indeed they were on their way to a paradise on earth.

She cleared her throat, smoothed out the folded letter, and began to read slowly and dramatically:

Avoca, Natal
29 January 1882

My darling Hellion,

This will likely be one of my last letters to you there in Kirrie from way out here in Natal. God willing, you will be leaving Scotland soon, so there will no longer be any need for us to correspond over time and distance like this on paper. Soon, soon I will see your lovely face again, hold you in my arms, bask in your glow, and drink in the dulcet sound of your voice and the fragrance of your skin and hair. My heart races at the thought of embracing you again!

But this writing paper has served its purpose well, hasn't it, my darling—acting as our faithful messenger-boy across the seas for these many weeks. And the paper I paint on, too, has been a fine companion in your absence. Wait until you see my sketchpad and the progress I've made with my artwork. My lines have become more sure, my perspectives have found greater depth and distance, my compositions are more balanced and pleasing to the eye, and my colours have begun to come to life, I like to think. I am learning the value of contrast—how the light is dependent on the dark.

I've learned so many things on my painting expeditions; among them, that the farthest hills in a landscape must always be depicted as hazy, the colour of bluish smoke. Like the future, they're not meant to be seen clearly. I've learned, too, that if all art has an underlying message or meaning, then mine tries to express both my awe and yearning—awe at God's breathtaking creation and yearning to capture it fully. I think I will always yearn to do so, while knowing full well I will never truly succeed.

I read a fine book the other day called Zulu-Land, by an American missionary who served here for several decades. One of his descriptions of this place is well worth quoting in full, my darling, because he writes far better than I ever could. This scene is from his first chapter, when he and a colleague were looking for a suitable location for his mission station, some forty miles north of Durban. The year was 1847:

> *And now, as the birds begin their joyous carol, mingling their sweet music with the song of the merry brook that flows at the foot of the hillock on which we have encamped, from the dark, low Zulu hut we emerge into bright light. We think that our eyes have*

seldom fallen upon a landscape of more native beauty. Looking along the hills and valleys that stretch out, up and down the country, covered as they now are with flowers of various hue and shape and grass of richest green, fragrant withal as a rose, we fancy we have found something like another Paradise, where "only man is vile."

Reading this made me glad that you and I have chosen to emigrate to South Africa instead of Australia or America. This distinguished American gentleman was well travelled, it seemed to me. If he considered this place to be one of the most beautiful on earth — "another Paradise," indeed!— then we have chosen wisely.

My work at the new station is going well. I am learning all I can about the Natal railways, and I continue to believe my future prospects are good. I have even memorized the train schedule so that I can be more readily helpful to anxious passengers and travelers. We have relatively few passengers now, but I am assured their numbers will rise as more immigrants arrive and spread out into the countryside. You and I will not be living in such an isolated area for long!

I wish you a safe and smooth journey, my darling. I know you can take care of yourself (Woe be unto anyone who tries to harm or trick my Hellion!), but my prayers will be with you every step of the way. Rest assured I will be there to meet you. You will recognize me in the crowd on the dock even from a great distance: I shall be the tall, thin, proud Scot with the broadest smile, the happiest man on earth to be seeing your face again.

Please give my fond regards to your family. I'm sure your mother is still cross with me for taking you so far away from her. I hope one day she will understand and forgive us both.

Godspeed!

Your loving husband, William

"Ahhhh, 'fragrant withal as a rose'!" one of Helen's listeners swooned. Another pressed both hands to the bodice of her nightdress and sighed, "Imagine! That American missionary thought South Africa is like paradise!" A third young woman admitted, "I wish I could find me a nice husband like your William. He seems t' be a prince."

Helen didn't share with the other women her husband's subsequent letters, in which his mood was beginning to darken and his patience was wearing thin. Instead, she kept these to herself and read them alone, knowing Will would soon be happy again.

Avoca, Natal, South Africa
11 February 1882

Dearest Hellion,

The weeks before your arrival seem like an eternity to me. The days are dragging. The heavy sun is moving more lazily than ever through the vast pale-blue sky. And the nights, especially, are interminably long. I wake in the blackness and listen for what seems like hours to the sounds outside — the wind shaking the trees' leaves, the nocturnal animals arguing among themselves, the birds softly cooing, as if in their sleep — all the while aching for you, my darling. How I wish I could force time to speed up, as with a crack of a whip on a horse's rump to make the buggy move faster!

Aye, you are right, I have not written much about my work because I haven't wanted to worry you. Really, there is nothing to worry about; but it is a concern to me that my supervisor is a difficult man and hard to please. Although I am doing my best to learn all that I can about this new railway business, he is quick to find fault with everything I do. It takes all my inner strength to hold my tongue, keep my head down like a beaten dog, and simply obey his never-ending orders. I thought I'd left this kind of man behind when I bid farewell to my father in Kirrie, but no. Here I am again, alas, face to face with a stern and unforgiving man who wields his paternalistic power with an iron hand.

And you would not want to see how harsh he is with the natives. He treats them with disdain and sometimes even threatens physical blows. But the Zulus here are a proud people; they don't take his guff. They stand tall and walk away, back to their villages. And they don't return.

As for me, I stay because I can see a future with the railway here. This bitter man will not last, I'm sure. He'll leave — go back to Liverpool or wherever he's from, or be killed mysteriously by a vengeful worker (not I!) — and then I'll be in line for a promotion. You can be sure I will certainly manage things differently.

In the meantime, I'm finding great solace in my painting, thanks to your inspired gift. On my days off from work, as I'm sure I've already told you, I walk far into the countryside, find a pleasant spot beneath a shady tree, and paint my worries away.

I've developed a system since I wrote to you last: First, I begin with a faint pencil sketch, drawing the scene in front of me to the best of my ability — the distant hills, the scraggy trees, the winding footpaths leading to unseen villages… Then I use a wide brush, laden with a light hue to "wash" the background — light, light blue for the overarching sky, pale brown for the wide, sunbaked veldt. After this "wash" dries, I take my time to colour in the scene I see before me, in successively darker shades. The watercolours create a misty effect, which is the way I see things in general, I suppose. Perhaps I require spectacles?

Finally, I try to add touches of detail, such as a branch in the foreground or far-off birds in flight. This last step is the hardest for me — taking the darkest colour of the lot and making the final, fine brush strokes that spell "The End" to the day's endeavors. Often, I am so transported by the act of painting, so lost in the beauty of the moment, I don't want the afternoon to come to a close.

I like to think that my artistic skills are gradually improving (well, at least they're not getting worse). It helps that I never strive to be perfect, as you know. Just "good enough" is good enough for me! That's a reasonable goal, don't you agree? This new pastime of mine is simply a great escape. All I hope to achieve is to capture moments in

Nature — the slant of the sunlight against that young tree, the odd, small, puff of a cloud that will never pass this way again.

After an afternoon spent walking and painting, I am renewed in body and spirit. I am able to return to work and face my supervisor without fear. He cannot harm me. I have Art (and "Uncle John") on my side!

That is all for now, my darling. Safe journey. God speed you to me!

Your own Michelangelo, William

The last letter Helen received from Will before her departure from Kirriemuir was the darkest. Helen had never known her sunny Will to be so despondent. He wrote,

> *…It's as if all of my pent-up feelings — loneliness, longing, frustration, hunger for your company — are seeping out of me, bleeding onto the paper, colours bleeding into other colours until the painting looks ugly and bears little resemblance to reality. It's as if in my impatience to be with you again I've lost my patience for painting, and my hasty efforts tell lies. The clear blue sky over the veldt that I see becomes overcast and sinister on my paper. The faint shadows cast by the willowy m'ssassa trees become black and ominous on the ground. The soft, bluish hills in the distance become large, dark and foreboding….*

But Helen knew that her arrival, their reunion, would cure his temporary ills. And her arrival would now be only a matter of days away.

Buoyed by hope and the forward momentum of the steamship, Helen's energies expanded and her own mood brightened. She wanted to dance and sing again; she wanted to share her joy and lift others' spirits too. So when she learned of an upcoming Passengers' Talent Night, she quickly agreed to participate.

She would sing the songs she'd sung at the community gatherings in Kirrie. She would pretend both Will and Jamie were there in the audience to applaud her. She would dance a little solo jig. She would pull the pins from her hair and let her long hair fly loose and free as she danced. She, Helen of Kirriemuir, single-handedly, would make everyone in attendance happy.

Atlantic Ocean, March 1882

Among the hundreds of passengers who, along with Helen David Black, boarded the Union Line steamship at Southampton that day bound for South Africa, was a lonely old classics professor named Clive Botha, heading to the Cape to visit his aged mother. This was a pilgrimage Professor Botha took every several years, during his sabbatical term from Oxford; it was a voyage and sojourn he both dreaded and treasured.

The dread for him came in the form of memories of his childhood at his parents' farm in the Cape Province. These memories overwhelmed him each time he stepped back onto his father's ancestral land. He had been a delicate, sickly, only child, overprotected by his bookish, birdlike British mother, and derided by his large, overbearing Boer father. His father had made his disappointment in his son plain: Why was he not growing up to be a manly man like himself, with a broad chest and a deep voice and strong arms? The boy had quivered in his father's presence and hid his thin, wan face in books.

Naturally, he escaped as soon as he could, finding his salvation in England and academia.

Now, decades later, now that his father was long dead and buried in the family plot, Professor Botha could treasure the moments he was able to share with his widowed mother alone. She was nearing ninety already and frail, cared for in her home by a staff of African servants long in her employ, and surrounded by old friends and neighbors who stopped by regularly to pay their respects and bring small, thoughtful gifts. But her son Clive was her greatest joy. And the look of adoration on her face when he walked in her front door after his long absence and vast ocean voyage was an expression that sustained him.

So he withstood the arduous journey again, knowing that it would not be long before his mother too would be buried beside her husband in the family plot. Two of the most unlikely people to ever have been married would be sleeping side by side for eternity. He shuddered at the thought.

He kept to himself on the ship. For the most part, he remained in his cabin and read or wrote. For him, stacks of books, sheaves of paper, clusters of pens, and bottles of ink were his lifelong closest friends. He "listened" to authors' voices; he "talked" to paper. He was alone, but seldom if ever considered himself as lonely. He loved his diary as though it were the sibling he never had.

Saturday morning
10 March 1882
(somewhere in the mid-Atlantic)

Until yesterday this voyage had been dull and uneventful and the weather a dismal grey. I had nothing good to report to you, so I didn't bother myself to write. Instead, I stayed in here reading, only occasionally going out to stand by the railing and watch the vast ocean roll past under an overcast sky. I wanted to command the ship to "Hurry it up!" in my sternest professorial voice, but I knew better of it.

The sameness of it all was beginning to wear on my nerves and make me weary — the same people going through their same motions with the same tired and anxious expressions on their sheet-white faces. Their faces seem to me to scream, What lies ahead?!

But then last night the tides changed, so to speak. Our young and accommodating crew organized the first of what they claim will be several talent shows, drawn from able volunteers, to entertain the listless guests. I attended this "opening night" performance with dubious expectations. After all, why have high hopes for such an amateur effort when you've seen the best that London has to offer? There is such as thing as jadedness, and I'll admit it is surely one of my many faults.

Well, to my great surprise, this show was the tonic. There was a fiddler who made toes tap, and a piper who brought tears to all the Scottish eyes. There were little twin girls with big bows in their hair who danced a lively jig while the audience clapped to keep time, and an elderly gent who fancied himself an opera baritone.

But one performer in particular captured my attention and has yet to let it go. I have not been able to get her out of my mind. Her beauty still haunts me. It is transcendent. The sound of her dulcet voice still rings in my ears. Everyone in the room — they used the dining hall for this first show — was enchanted by her singing, not just me. No one stirred or made a sound as she sang. Her voiced seemed to touch hearts and soothe souls, including my own.

Now I know I must seek out this young woman and speak to her. I must learn who she is and why she is here on this voyage. Such a voice — such beauty — belongs on the London stage, not confined to a low ceilinged, wood-paneled room on a steamship bound for the southernmost tip of darkest Africa!

Yes, her beauty haunts me. It is as if I have seen her face before, but I cannot recall where. Am I losing my mind? My mind is all that I have left! Dear me.

Today I will put down my books and try to find her. I now have a quest. But I will be discreet. My purpose, I must make clear to her, is not romantic. After all, I am clearly old enough to be her father — or grandfather! No, I must convey that I am merely an admirer, perhaps a potential mentor. I must let her know that she has brightened an otherwise dreary trip — for me, as well as all the other weary passengers. I must see her again, and she must sing again! And soon!

Wednesday evening
14 March 1882
(further south in the Atlantic)

*It's been some days since I last wrote to you, dear
diary. In this period my preoccupation has been in tracking
down the mysterious chanteuse of the talent show. I asked
everyone I could comfortably approach: "Do you know who
that lovely young singer is? Do you know how I might be
introduced to her?" I must say I was met with some raised
eyebrows, as though all grey-haired men in tweed suits
traveling the world alone were suspect.*

*"She is a married woman, Professor," one steward told
me firmly.*

*"I can assure you, young man," I said to him, with as
much indignity as I could muster, "my intentions are quite
pure. I only want to speak with her."*

At last, he agreed to make the arrangements.

*This afternoon she and I had our first conversation —
outdoors, on deck chairs, in full view of everyone near the
steerage section where she is staying. It was, after long last,
a balmy day; the sun had broken through the clouds, lifting everyone's spirits. Children frolicked in the newfound
sunshine, under the watchful eyes of their anxious young
mothers, who shouted warnings over the noisy waves, "Don't
go near the railings, Johnny!" — or James, or Sarah — or
whatever their children's names.*

*My heart is still aflutter after this first, face-to-face
encounter. No, I wouldn't call it love — I'm too old and*

withered for even the hope of that now. It's more like I've swallowed a butterfly quite by chance, and the sensation is both new and absurd to me. How else to describe this wild and winged thing inside?

When she looked at me with those probing, blue-green eyes, I was left nearly speechless. Her long, honey-golden hair was tied back in a knot at the nape of her neck today, unlike the way she wore it when she'd performed, loose and free. She was withdrawn at first, seemingly wary of me, as though she is experienced at guarding herself against advancing men. When she smoothed her skirt or touched the high collar of her blouse, I couldn't help but admire her strong-yet-feminine expressive hands and her long, tapered fingers.

And then I realized where I had seen her face and hands before! She is the image of my friend Gabriel Rossetti's painting of Helen of Troy. He had used that English barmaid Annie Miller, his then-lover, as his model for this painting in 1863, after his wife's suicide. But his vision of the demigoddess Helen of Troy, as proven in his painting, was far more beautiful than that lowly barmaid Annie ever was, and I told him so myself. The thought crossed my mind that I should write to him and tell him about this girl— "Your Helen of Troy lives, old boy!" But I'm sure that would kill him, if he's not dead already. Last I heard he was in a morbid state, brought low by his long addiction to chloral hydrate and whisky. Ah, artists are indeed a complicated lot.

Well, diary, you can imagine my surprise when I learned that this girl's name is Helen. I must have exhibited such shock at learning this that she felt the need to prove her name to me. She showed me the embroidery on the lovely white shawl she had wrapped loosely over her shoulders. "Helen David of Kirriemuir" the blue embroidery read.

"Kirriemuir?" was all I could think to say aloud, while in my mind I thought, "No, Helen of Troy." She explained, as though I were an old fool and not an Oxford don (but perhaps I am both by now) that Kirriemuir is a small village in Angus, Scotland, noted for its linen weaving.

"Oh?" I said, unable to take my eyes off of her perfect face. "Aren't you rather young to run away?"

She said she is nineteen and has been a married woman for five months. She's on her way to join her husband in Natal, where they plan to make a new life.

She has, it appears, no fears for the future.

What a brave and headstrong woman she is, I thought, traveling alone across the seas so fearlessly!

When at last I regained my ability to converse, I asked whether she knew the story of Helen of Troy, whose face, it was claimed, had had the power to "launch a thousand ships." She looked at me blankly. Of course, how could I have expected that anyone from such a little burgh could be well educated? So I told her the myth, in brief: Helen, a daughter of Zeus, was the most beautiful woman in Greece — if not the world — at that time. Although married to the king of Sparta, she ran off with — or, some say, was carried off by — Paris, a handsome prince of Troy, while her husband Menelaus was away on business. "Throughout history she has been blamed for the ten-year-long Trojan War that ensued," I told Helen of Kirriemuir. "But I believe she was just a pawn of the gods and of powerful men."

Clearly, this Helen didn't know what to make of me. Was I merely a crazed codger, a lonely old bachelor professor who'd lost his moorings out at sea? She listened to my lecture politely, her hands folded tightly in her lap, her eyes searching my face for signs of madness. She accepted my comparison of her with the beautiful and immortal Helen of Troy without any sign of emotion.

"Will you be performing again?" I said finally. "I hope you will sing again for us." She said she would like that, and then, at last, she smiled.

* * *

Saturday morning
17 March 1882
(nearing the Cape)

Helen of Kirriemuir sang again last night to a full and rapturous audience of passengers and crew. She sang mostly Scottish ballads, which tugged at hearts and brought the soft sound of sniffles to the room. Unlike me, who's made this voyage many times before, the other passengers are floating in a kind of limbo, having let go of their homeland and not yet reached their "promised land." I feel for them. The reality of life in South Africa, which I long ago abandoned, will for some of these anxious passengers be a bitter pill.

For the moment, though, Helen's songs provide an outlet, a kind of communal catharsis. The audience, I observed, *looks upon this Helen as if she were a godsend — or even a goddess! (A daughter of Zeus!) Her voice, indeed, seems to come from another sphere, another world altogether. How can so much latent talent exist in someone so young, so unpracticed, so untrained?*

I sat close to the front and studied her, recording in my mind her every musical note and phrase. And I was able to note that her likeness to Rossetti's painting is more than astounding: The long, flowing, golden hair; the large, wide-set, blue-green eyes; the fine nose, full lips, and strong jaw, plus the expressive hands fingering her beaded neck-lace. If Rossetti were here on this voyage, he would not believe his eyes!

But it is what I recall in the background of Rossetti's painting of Helen of Troy that disturbs me: Troy is ablaze. Behind that beautiful Helen is a scene of smoke and flames. She, however, filling the foreground, is looking only for-ward. She appears oblivious to what is encroaching. Or is it that she is resigned? Her facial expression is inscrutable.

At first I wanted this ship to hasten on its way, and now I want it to slow to a crawl. Soon I will be disem-barking in Cape Town, and I will likely never see this living Helen of Troy again in my lifetime. I am more grateful to her than she will ever know for the happiness she brought me on this trip. I had thought my heart was too old to flutter like a schoolboy's. This lovely Helen has proved me wrong.

Taos, New Mexico, Summer 2012

Although it's from a distance of more than one hundred and thirty years, I can see her clearly: getting off the ship, searching for Will among the others on the quay, lifting her long skirt with one hand and clutching her small satchel in the other, running toward him, the way she'd run after the train at Kirrie station that had taken him away from her nearly four months before. There, she had run in the cold and snow; now she runs in embracing warmth and sunlight. There, there were pine trees; here there are palm trees. This is another world.

And has it only been four months that they have been apart? For Helen it seems like four years. She promises herself they will never be separated by anything again. She runs to him as if she were dancing to the music of life, the beat of her heart, sure-footed and gracefully, without bumping into anyone — dodging obstacles, mindless of the midday sun and enveloping heat. I see people stepping away and smiling, understanding her youthful, passionate urgency.

And I can see William, too, standing frozen in place, the way he'd stood at the altar in Southmuir on his wedding day, too nervous to run or even move, numb with joy, as he watches Helen approach like a winged angel dressed in blue. Will's sun-bronzed arms are folded at his chest in an effort to keep his pounding heart from bursting through his ribcage. His legs feel grounded, as if by some magic he'd been turned into a sturdy tree with deep roots.

"Will, Will!" Helen calls as she swoops into his open arms. He holds her close and breathes the sweet fragrance of her hair and skin. They are together again.

And now I project: Helen's experience of Africa in the years that she lived there was exactly like my own; we are, of course, closely connected by blood, DNA, and sun sign. She, like me, loved the never-ending warmth and sunshine; the tropical foliage; the unbroken blue sky; the rich, elemental earthiness of the terrain. She was fascinated by the diversity of the people, dressed in strange attire and speaking unfathomable languages: small, shy, dark men dressed in white, brought from India to work on the sugar plantations outside of Durban; tall, dignified, scantily clad black Africans — mostly Zulus, she was told — who walked like royalty; burly Boer farmers in worn-out work clothes, slouch hats and thick beards who moved furtively and spoke gutturally; and British colonials with pale skin, wide eyes and welcoming smiles whose regional accents pinpointed their place of origin — southern England, northern England, Ireland, Wales, Scotland.

Helen loved the largeness of it all, that this faraway spot on the globe should attract and embrace such differences in humanity. Not like little Kirriemuir with its sameness in everything — the way people spoke and dressed and ate and lived and even thought; always the same narrow little winding roads under the same chilly, nearly-always-overcast skies. Here in Africa Helen felt free to be herself and do as her heart led her. There was no one and nothing to stop her. Certainly not Will. He would have sooner stopped the tide.

Yes, I can see them making a homestead in Avoca, in the place that Will had found for them. I can see the lacy curtains Helen made by hand, sheer enough to let the sunlight in. I can see her kitchen garden and her neat rows of corn and squash.

I know she loved to cook. And to make love. In their "honeymoon suite" at Strath View, they'd had to be quiet in bed so as not to disturb or alarm Jamie Barrie's family. But here in their own, isolated cabin, they could make love every night with no thought of others overhearing, and no inhibitions.

I can see Will riding to his work at the Avoca station on his very own "iron horse," a bicycle he'd bought second-hand and loved as if it were alive. I can see him in the evening at their wooden table, drawing and painting Helen's face by lamplight. As he paints she tells him about the old professor on the ship — she thinks his name was Botha — who told her she looked like a painting by a friend of his, the artist Rossetti.

"Oh, *really?*" Will asks, pretending to be jealous.

"Yes," she says. "The painting is titled Helen of Troy."

"Well, then, I'll paint my own Helen of Troy," he says, intently returning to his brush strokes.

Will had, of course, followed through on his promise to sketch the stone Helen had so lovingly chosen and carefully carried from Kirriemuir. He had, in fact, done a number of drawings of the small, star-flecked, black stone and set them on their mantelpiece in a row, like the cars of a train. He proudly called it his "Lucky Stone Rail Line," which made Helen smile.

Sometimes he painted still lifes made of fresh vegetables from their garden, such as an ear of African corn with some small African pumpkins and gourds in a pile on the table. Once, Helen enclosed one of these still lifes in a letter to her mother with a note about her beloved garden. "But it's a good thing Will doesn't paint my hands," she wrote to Agnes, "because all this gardening has made them rough and brown!"

I can see Helen at the Avoca community center when they held a talent night. I see her singing. But the response of this audience is mixed. The men, of course, admire her; but some of the women whisper among themselves:

"Well, she thinks very highly of herself, doesn't she."

"She's not very friendly. She never comes to tea."

"I hear she's friendly with the natives, though. *Tsk-tsk.*"

I can see this, too: One day in about September 1884, a young Zulu woman came to their veranda looking for work. By this time, Helen was three months' pregnant. She had had a series of miscarriages already, so the local doctor had strongly advised her to stay close to home and "take it easy if you want to keep this baby." The Zulu girl's arrival was well timed. Helen could use her help.

Her name was Amma. She was tall and lithe, like Helen, with fine features, a regal bearing, and strong, capable hands. Will joked that she and Helen looked like they could be sisters — from different fathers, of course. Amma sensed this, too, but she saw Helen as albino, like one of her own half-sisters in her village.

Amma didn't know her exact age, but they guessed she was about sixteen. She spoke little English, but she was quick to learn.

Just as I had done with my African women friends when I lived and worked in Africa among Africans for years, Helen and Amma learned from each other. Ignoring the colonials' inclination to treat Africans as inferiors, Helen valued Amma's friendship. She learned some words in Zulu. She sought Amma's gardening counsel. They shared each other's songs and dances. Helen taught Amma how to dance a jig. And, yes, together they got work done. On William and Helen's small homestead, in preparation for their baby's arrival, there was much work to do.

Zululand, March 1885

On the day that Amma, one of the chief's many children by his several wives, ran from Helen's house, Amma's half-sister Themba was nursing her dying mother in their hut. Themba was eighteen by then, with a precarious future ahead of her. She knew no one would marry her. No man in the kraal, young or old, would dare to marry a ghost who would, in turn, produce ghost children. Without her mother, she would have no one.

As she wiped her mother's brow, then lifted her mother's head from the wooden headrest to try to spoon-feed her some milky cornmeal gruel, Themba could only feel a sense of foreboding. She prayed to Great-Great for strength and purpose.

Themba's mother, the chief's first wife, had given her albino baby girl the name Themba, which meant "hope," at birth, hoping that her daughter, her first child, would not remain the color of milk. She prayed fervently that Unkulunkulu, Great-Great, would give her child the same rich, dark-brown color as all the other children in the kraal. She prayed that this child would not grow up to be a living ghost, an aberration and outcast.

But Themba's mother's prayers for her daughter were never answered as she'd hoped. The little girl never gained colorfulness. Her pale blue eyes never adapted to Africa's fierce sunlight. She was shunned by everyone, including her own father, who refused to believe that he, the great chief, known as "the one who is blackest," should produce a child with no color, no value, at all. He did not demand the bride price back, but he never again visited Themba's mother's hut in the night as his wife. He turned to his other wives instead.

Despite the chief's rejection, Themba's mother loved and protected her frail, pale, child. She kept the little girl indoors in their hut, shielded from the piercing sun and the fearsome stares of the others. She kept the child busy, polishing the floor with smooth stones, and grinding corn on a large, flat stone. She taught her how to string colorful beads and weave sturdy reed mats. She taught her songs and told her stories. Sometimes they even danced together, pounding their bare feet and clapping their hands in the privacy of their own beehive-shaped hut.

Themba's mother knew there were those in the clan, even the child's own half-brothers, who would, if given a chance, readily exile her daughter — take her into the bush one night and leave her there for the lions and hyenas to tear apart by moonlight — because they believed she was destined to bring them all bad luck.

That would not happen, Themba's mother resolved, as long as she herself was alive to protect her daughter.

It was close to sunset when Amma arrived at the kraal, panting and perspiring from running many miles, tightly clutching the baby boy wrapped in Helen's soft, white linen shawl. She had run barefoot, frightened that the men on horseback might chase her down too. She ran as fast as the wind, across the grassy veldt, through the valley, over the time-softened hills, following the sinking sun, until she reached her own village, where she knew she and the baby would be safe, protected by her warrior brothers, cousins, and uncles.

Her sudden arrival caused a commotion. "What is this?" the people asked one another when they saw Amma enter, holding a bundle wrapped in white cloth in her arms. Yet they stood aside, respectfully, to let Amma approach her father's hut. They could see that this was a grave matter, which only the chief could adjudicate.

Themba peered out of the low door of her hut to see what was causing the commotion. Everyone was gathering outside the chief's hut. "Why?" she wondered. "What is happening?" When she returned to her mother, she saw that her mother's spirit had left her. Her mother's heart was no longer beating, her nostrils were no longer taking in or giving out air. Themba was all alone in the world for the first time in her life. In a daze, she crawled out of the door of her hut and walked across the courtyard toward the gathering crowd to tell the chief of her mother's passing. The sun had fallen beneath the horizon, so Themba had no need to squint and shield her pale blue eyes.

Breathlessly, Amma tried to explain to the chief what had happened to Helen and William. "Three men arrived on horseback," she said, "while mister was working in the garden, raking and burning brush, the way I had shown him how, and missus was nursing the baby indoors."

"What kind of men?" asked the chief. "Were they dressed in red coats?"

"No," Amma answered. "They wore ragged farmers' clothes and cloth hats. They were young. Fat. And drunk." She imitated their drunken, belligerent behavior, shouting at William in slurred, guttural English and calling him names Amma didn't understand. "Mister's two dogs started to growl and bare their teeth. The chickens began to squawk loudly and run in circles. One of the men shot both dogs and some of the chickens. I ran inside. The drunken men laughed.

"Missus and I watched from the window. Mister dropped his rake and approached the men with his hands up, to make peace, but the leader of the bad men struck him down with the butt of his rifle. Mister shouted to missus, 'Take the baby and run, Helen!' But, no! Missus wrapped the baby in this," Amma said, stroking the linen shawl, "and gave him to me to take to my village for safety. And then she picked up mister's rifle hanging above the door and went out onto the front veranda and aimed it at the bad men."

Amma stopped to catch her breath. The baby in her arms began to fret.

"I ran out the back way," she said. "I heard the shots and then the missus' loud screams. 'No!' the missus screamed. 'No! NO!' And then more shots. I ran and ran. When I turned and looked back, I saw the fire and smoke. So much fire! So much smoke!…" Amma's voice caught in her throat.

"They are gone," she added softly, as she tried to comfort the bundled baby.

The chief shook his head. "We cannot keep this child," he said. "It will bring great trouble to us if he is found here. They will think we have stolen him."

It was a Zulu custom, Amma knew, to steal a child from the enemy before going to war, and then offering the stolen child as a sacrifice to the spirits to obtain their favor and insure victory.

Knowing she could not argue with her father, Amma did her best to gently convince him that this situation was different. "This was his mother's last wish, Father," she said.

The chief raised his braceleted arm to signal silence. He had allowed his brightest daughter, Amma, to work for the ghost-people because he'd wanted her to learn their language and tell him of their mysterious ways. Why were so many coming to this land? What did they want? What were they willing to give in exchange? Now this. The ghost-baby in Amma's arms began to cry a hungry cry. Amma put her thumb in the baby's mouth to quiet him.

Fortunately, another of the chief's daughters, his blackest, most beautiful and most favored child, witnessed this scene and took Amma's side. "Father," she said, "the baby is here now. Great-Great has brought him to us. We can care for him until we are shown another plan."

Outside the chief's hut, the people parted to let Themba through. Timidly, she approached her father to announce her mother's death. When the chief's favored daughter heard Themba's news, she knew she'd found the solution. "Father," she continued, "let us put this white baby in Themba's care. If any strangers come and see him, they will think he is hers."

"Give him to her," the chief ordered Amma, gruffly indicating that she hand the baby over to Themba's outstretched arms. And to Themba he said, "See that he gets fed."

When Themba unwrapped the baby and looked closely into his eyes, eyes that were blue like her own, she felt the full force of an overpowering emotion she'd only known toward her mother: Love. This white baby was her baby, a miracle, an answer to prayers. On this day Great-Great had taken her mother from her but in exchange had given her this child. She put the baby on her back and wrapped him firmly around her body with Helen's linen shawl. Later, she named the baby Umnikelo Tande, meaning Gift of Love.

"His name is John," Amma corrected her.

Themba wouldn't listen. To her, he was Tande.

Natal, April 1885

News of the incident flared up then died down quickly in Natal, like a small brush fire. The newspaper had called it a "tragic accident," a garden fire that had burned out of control due to sudden, changing winds. The young couple, who had emigrated from Scotland only a few years before, the paper reported, were obviously still unaware of the unpredictability of Natal's weather. The brief newspaper report became a terse cautionary tale for naive new immigrants: Pay close attention to Africa's weather, and don't use brush fires to clear your land, as the backward Africans do.

If there had been an investigation into this "accident," the newspaper didn't report it. If the authorities had immediately sifted through the charred remains of Helen and William's small, remote homestead, they might have seen some black, blood-soaked earth and found the bullets in what little was left of the couple's bodies as well as the dogs'. They might have looked more closely for evidence of the baby's death.

But the fire had burned hot, extinguishing most

traces of the truth. The killers, who knew the land and the weather and the unspoken fears and apprehensions of the new, British immigrants, had counted on the fire to obliterate their sins. If any of these brutish young men had read the newspaper's report of the young couple and their infant son perishing in this tragic, accidental fire, they would have laughed out loud and slapped one another on the back.

They rationalized among themselves: She shot first. They felt justified, even victorious; after all, their people had always been at war with the British.

No one even bothered to look for possible treasure amidst the charred rubble. If someone had, he might have found the gold-plated pocket watch William's father had given Will on his departure from Kirriemuir, engraved with his own initials, "J.B." Helen's treasured smooth, black, oval stone—with its speckles of white like the stars in the night sky—would have gone unnoticed. Who would care about a worthless stone? The sketches of it and the other stones on the mantle would have been reduced to ashes, along with Will's sketchbook. And Will's charred, thin, tin paint box would have held no value to anyone.

People talked, as they will do, especially the local ladies when they next gathered for tea.

"Oh, what a sorry shame!" said one.

"She was such a lovely girl," said another.

"Didn't she sing sweetly at the meeting hall?" remarked another.

"Like a bird," said the first. "A bird of paradise."

"How do you know what birds of paradise sound like?" said her friend beside her.

"And her husband was so handsome," said another dreamily. "What was his name?"

"William Black, I think."

"Oh, yes, he was the station master at Avoca, wasn't he?"

"I've never had occasion to use the train. We travel to Durban in our buggy."

"There is a portrait he did, hanging in the meeting hall. It is of a beautiful young woman. His wife, I believe. Lovely girl."

"I must look for it the next time I'm there."

"He was a Freemason, wasn't he?"

"I have no idea."

"They're very secretive, aren't they?"

"They say."

"I hadn't seen his wife for some time."

"Not very friendly, was she."

"She was confined to bed rest during the last months of her pregnancy. The doctor didn't want her to lose another baby, I was told."

"Had she miscarried before?"

"Yes. At least twice. Or so I heard."

"Oh."

"Such a sorry shame."

"Yes. A shame."

"Too bad he didn't know how to control the fire."

"I'm glad my husband is good at such things."

"So am I!"

"Yes."

"Tsk-tsk."

"Lovely girl."

"Yes."

"More tea?"

Kirriemuir, May 1885

When the dreadful news reached Kirriemuir, Agnes
at first refused to believe it. She had almost finished
knitting a sweater for her first grandchild, whom Helen
and William had named John. The little sweater was
blue, soft and light. Knitting it had become a true labor
of love for Agnes because every stitch pained her. Her
gnarled, arthritic hands rebelled against the needles'
demands. Nevertheless, she stubbornly persevered. This
gift, she resolved, would be unspoken proof of her love,
devotion, and, indeed, sacrifice.

"Africa is cool at night sometimes," Helen had
reported in a letter, so a baby sweater was in order.

Helen's letters had been so full of life and happiness and sunshine. She had loved her new life in South
Africa — her "heart's home," she had called it — with
all its simple, homey, pastoral pleasures. She especially
loved her small cottage with its shaded front veranda,
and her small flock of clucking chickens who followed
her like ducklings, and her burgeoning kitchen garden.
She had written to Agnes often of her joy in watching

the seeds she'd carefully planted spring to verdant life. And of her even greater joy in experiencing the new life that was growing inside her own body.

My Helen canna' be dead! Agnes insisted. *No, God wouldna' allow such a thing. They've made a mistake. William wasna' careless lad. No, William was as steady and sure as a train schedule! This couldna' been his fault.* This terrible accident had happened to other people, not her family.

Agnes picked up and reread the letter she had just written but had not yet mailed:

My Bonny Lass,

Whenever we have a clear day, when there are patches of blue sky between the clouds, I think of the blue skies you write of in your letters. Is it the same sky we're both lookin' at, I wonder to mysel'? You over there in Africa, so far away from your true home, and me in the same place as you left me three long years ago? I look to the sky for answers. Are the cottony clouds listenin'? Is there a God lurkin' behind 'em, seein' my old face and hearin' my prayers for you night and day? Added to my aches and pains and back bent from the loom and my knotted hands are my worries for your safety there. What is a mother to do?

This letter, like all the others she'd written to her daughter, contained town news and gossip, complaints about her son Davey and her husband Sandy's behavior, and pleas for Helen's safe return. And it closed, as usual, with:

My writin' hand is painin' me now. I'll ask your brother to rewrite this letter for me in his clearer hand and correct my err's. He's a good one for a' that! Tomorrow, then, he will take it to the post for me. He will smile sweetly at ol' Lizzie and tell her all that I've said to you, to save her the trouble of steamin' the letter open.

With luck and godspeed, this letter should be reachin' you in a few weeks' time. Take care o' yoursel' and your William and the wee bonny bairn!—Your lovin' Mum.

Agnes felt dizzy and confused. Should she mail the letter? Of course, she should. They've made a mistake. Helen and William and their new baby boy were alive and well. But why did she get this awful news? How could they have made such a cruel error? Who could she turn to? Her husband Sandy, seemingly in shock at the news, took his gun and went hunting with Davey, where they would unleash their anger and sorrow by killing lesser animals.

Agnes was alone in the cottage where Helen had grown up, had toddled and danced and strutted and slept and laughed and cried and sang. Echoes of her daughter's lovely voice reverberated through the small space. It wasn't possible that that voice had been silenced by death. This news couldn't be true.

When the rest of Kirriemuir heard the news and shared their condolences with Helen's family, Agnes affected appreciation, but in her heart she was enraged. And as soon as Sandy and Davey returned home, empty-handed, she turned her anger on them. Somehow, she expected them to fix things, to make it all right — *Isn't that wha' men should be good at?!*

She wanted them to let everyone in Kirrie know that Helen and William and the baby hadn't died in South Africa. Oh, no! A mistake had been made. "Tell them!" she shouted at her son and husband, "so they'll stop sayin' 'We're so sorry…' I canna' bear to hear their pityin' words any longer!" She clapped her hands against her ears and howled at the rafters of their cottage. Davey reached out to stroke his mother's back to soothe her, while Sandy left their home again without saying a word.

Davey, a full-grown man by now, tried to gently reason with his mother. He pointed out that the letter from David Hunter, general manager of the Natal Government Railways, written on his company's stationery, could not have been a mistake. Mr. Hunter had expressed his "profound sorrow" at this loss, his "great admiration" for young William Black and his charming wife Helen, his "deepest condolences" to their families in Scotland, his own homeland.

But Agnes could only moan, like a huge wounded animal. Her thick, twisted hands clawed the air desperately. She shook her head in disbelief and pulled away from her son. Her breaking heart was beyond the reach of reason.

Will's father, too, had received the same kind letter from Hunter following the shocking brief telegram announcing the "tragic accident." Sitting in his favorite chair by the hearth in his cottage, he read the railway manager's letter again and again, until he had memorized every word. Then he tossed the letter into the fireplace and watched it burn, folding in on itself like a slowly clenching hand, until it fell to pieces in the ashes.

John Black, who had only recently felt rare joy at the news that his only grandchild had been named John, after himself he'd presumed, sat back in his chair, studied the flames, and considered his life: It too had turned to ashes.

In the South Parish Church in Southmuir, the same church where Helen and William had been married close to four years before, the Reverend Alexander Duff, who had officiated at their wedding, gave a moving sermon at their memorial service. The small church was filled with mourners: Mr. James Wilkie of the linen factory and his wife; Mr. William Mills, the printer and publisher, and his family; the widowed postmistress, Lizzie, who made it her business to know all the news; Helen's former co-workers, some of whom were married now and mothers themselves; the elderly villagers who'd delighted in Helen's singing and dancing at town gatherings; William's many admirers from his days at the Kirrie railway station; Jamie Barrie's spinster sister Jane Ann, taking a break from caring for her mother; and of course William's father and Helen's parents and brother.

Reverend Duff spoke of love and loss. He reminded the congregation of the brightness of this young couple,

whom God had taken home to be with Him. "They—
and their sweet baby whom none of us had ever seen—
are safe now in the Lord's house," Duff said. "It is we
who ache and weep and shout at God— *Why? Why???*"

Duff went on to imply that God in His wisdom
may prefer that his children "grow where He has planted them"; that is, stay close to home. "Unless we receive
a clear call to serve as a missionary in the Lord's work in
far-off lands, it may be better to serve him right here at
home," he said. He meant well, they knew, by suggest-
ing everyone there should live and die in Kirriemuir and
be safely buried in the town's Hill Cemetery overlooking
the beautiful, wide, green valley. But some in the congregation also detected a hint of blame in what he said,
as though Helen and William had brought this tragedy
upon themselves by being young, rash and impetuous.
Africa! Indeed.

Agnes, sitting between her husband and her son
in a front pew, used all the strength she could command
to hold her head up and her tears in. *They willna' see me
weep,* she repeated to herself, and to God she seethed,
How could you do this?! How could you?! She hadn't
heard a word of Duff's eulogy. Instead, she'd thought
of Queen Victoria, always dressed in black since her
beloved husband Albert died more than twenty years
before. Yes, she, Agnes Reid David, felt a kinship with
Queen Victoria for the first time in her life. She too
would wear only black from now on. There were no
more colors in her world.

"Gracious God," Reverend Duff intoned in his closing prayer, "we cannot know the mysteries of your ways. Our lives are journeys of faith. Help us to trust. Help us to accept your will for us and not wander off…"

John Black, dressed in the same black suit he'd worn to bid farewell to Will at the Kirrie station in late 1881 (the only suit he owned), made a silent vow never to enter the doors of any church ever again in what was left of his life. This was a vow he would staunchly keep.

After that day, few if any young people from Kirriemuir dared to leave home to make new lives for themselves in the colonies. Instead, they silently swore to safely spend their entire lives in Kirrie and be buried right there on the Hill, where Helen and William could not be buried. There had been no remains to send home.

Jamie Barrie received the news of Helen's death in Bloomsbury, London, where he'd moved that March to begin climbing the ladder of literary fame. He had arrived with only £12 in his pocket, but with a mind overflowing with creative ideas and a heart filled with hope for his eventual success.

His lodging, on Greville Street, near the British Museum and its beloved Reading Room, was "not much larger than a piano case," he'd written to Helen in a recent letter. It had only one window, which overlooked a sooty, blank wall with a spindly tree in between. He stood at that window now with the letter from his sister Jane Ann shaking in his hands, his mind and heart suddenly engulfed in guilt and sorrow. He had never felt so bereft in his life.

It's all my fault, he told himself repeatedly, as he paced the room.

He resolved to bury himself—his heart, his soul, his mind—in his work. He would bury himself alive.

Zululand, 1888

It was a time of peace. The warriors had not had occasion to bloody their spears since well before Amma had arrived with the ghost baby wrapped in his dead mother's cloth. Two mild and sunny winters and two hot and rain-blessed summers had passed. The corn and yam harvests had been abundant, miraculously unharmed by wayward elephants and ravenous wild boars. There had been many reasons for the people to rejoice, including two wedding feasts.

Already Themba's love, Tande, was walking by her side and speaking words in the musical Zulu language. He would point to himself and say *"umfana"* (boy) or to the prized cattle penned within the circular thorny fence at the center of the kraal and say *"inkomo"* (cow). He called Themba, as well as all the loving young mothers who had suckled him before he was weaned, by the name *"umame"* (my mother).

In this peaceful time the warriors occupied themselves with domestic chores — digging earthen pits for storing grain, rethatching their beehive-shaped huts that

encircled the central cow-pen, or repairing and reinforc-
ing the kraal's high outer circular fencing with stakes
and thorny bushes to protect against predators. The
men also assisted in choosing the best site for the newest
insimu (garden), near a stream that was only a relatively
short walk from the kraal, then cutting away the thick
brush so the women could plant there.

The women and girls, each with a basket of seed
on her head, would then proceed with their designated
tasks — scattering the seeds under the burning sun, after
hoeing the earth to mellow it and prepare it to bring
forth food to support their families and community.
Their day's work done, the women would then return
home, carrying bundles of wood picked up along the
way, to fuel their outdoor cook-fires. While the wom-
en prepared their family's principal meal, the children
ran to the stream to fill calabashes with fresh water. At
sunset the men, women, and children gathered together
to eat by their fires.

Themba's colorless, ghostlike skin and pale, weak
eyes prevented her from being outdoors in daylight and
working in the fields with the other women under Africa's unremitting sun. Instead, she was allowed, like the
very elderly and infirm, to stay behind in the kraal and
remain, for the most part, indoors. There, in the privacy
and quietude of her hut, Themba showered her Tande
with all the love she possessed. She smiled at him and
sang to him, the same songs her mother had sung to
her when she was young. She stroked his soft, smooth,

straight hair — hair that so reminded her of corn silk she couldn't bear to cut it, so she let it grow long like a girl's.

In the early days after Great-Great had given her this infant, and the chief, Themba's father, had ordered him fed, young mothers who had hitherto shunned Themba, believing she would bring them all bad luck, visited her hut with their own babies to share their breast milk with Themba's ghost-child. They came dutifully at first, with long faces and slumped shoulders, reaching out to bring this hungry white child to their breast as though this were just one more burden in their already heavily burdened lives. But soon enough, that all changed.

Themba prepared the interior of her hut as though it were a palace. She pounded and rubbed her earthen floor with smooth stones until it shone like polished ebony. She laid out clean, woven mats for her new visitors to sit on. She fanned them with a round, reed fan she'd made, to cool them and keep the flies at bay. She kept separate calabashes filled with luxurious thickened sour milk, water, and corn-beer, offering whichever the mothers requested. She entertained their children while the mothers breast fed her Tande.

She told stories — the same stories her mother used to tell her — to amuse them all. She gave the women gifts of thin, beaded cowhide bracelets she'd made to thank them. She pampered them and flattered them and made them happy in every way she could.

Before long the mothers began to visit Themba's hut willingly and happily, and they grew to love Themba's plump, hungry ghost-child — and the pale, slender Themba too. They began to see beneath their milk-white skin.

Amma, whose wedding feast had been a recent cause for rejoicing among everyone in the community, was not yet a mother, but she came to visit Themba and the baby almost daily. She called Tande "John" and rocked him in her arms the way she remembered Helen doing. And she tried her best to recall some of the songs Helen used to sing.

"OhmyluvizlikearrrrredrrrrredROSE!" she crooned to the baby, who looked back at her, bewildered.

"Hello, John," Amma said, in an effort to teach him what little English she remembered. "Floor," she said, patting Themba's mirror-like floor. "Basket," she said, pointing to one of Themba's many ornate hand-made reed baskets. "Food," she said, offering him his first solid food, mashed stewed pumpkin mixed with mealies, cornmeal mush, held in a small calabash bowl.

She told him, in Zulu, even though he was far too young to understand, the story of his birth: How she, Amma, and his father, "mister," had, together, brought him into this world at their homestead because he wanted to arrive early, before there was time to get the doctor; how brave his mother Helen had been — just like an African woman, she did not cry out while birthing but rather gritted her teeth; how small and blue

he was at first, but when she, Amma, spanked him —
lovingly — he had cried a cry that said I AM HERE! and
then he was all right and mister was so relieved!

When Themba was not within earshot, Amma told
him often, too, about his real mother, his "blood mother,"
Helen: How she tried to learn to speak Zulu and loved
to garden and sang almost all day long and taught Amma
how to dance a jig. Amma tried to explain that Helen
was now with Great-Great in heaven; and Themba had
become his new mother, his "love mother." The boy
listened quizzically while Amma fed him his porridge.

In the relative cool of the evening, after the sun had
fallen beneath the horizon on the western rim of their
world, Themba was free to wrap her baby on her back
with Helen's linen shawl and proudly walk with him
around the kraal. Because of her newfound friendships
with so many young mothers, people now greeted her
kindly and some invited her to join their family's meal.
Their sense of *ubuntu* (sharing) now extended to her,
even though she still appeared ghost-like. The children,
knowing her from their pleasant times in her hut, no
longer taunted her; the men, influenced by their wives,
no longer threatened her. She was a mother now, a real
woman. She was, except for her unfortunate white skin
and pale blue eyes and the fact that she lived alone with
a dead ghost-woman's baby, almost normal.

When her Tande was small, Themba wrapped him
close to her slim back, so that only his tiny white feet

123

protruded from the linen wrapping on both sides of her waist. But then as he grew, his head, shoulders and arms protruded too, and the people, now protective of Themba and her baby, warned her of the dangers.

"He must not be seen by outsiders," one person warned.

"They will know by his corn silk hair that he is not yours and he is not ours," another added.

"They will take him away," said a third, "and you will never see him again."

Themba pretended she didn't hear them. She had heard unkind words directed at her for most of her life. They had said she was bad luck. They had called her bewitched. They said ghosts don't die, they just disappear. One young man had threatened to skin her alive and use her albino skin for magic potions. She had learned how to deflect words that could pierce like spears.

She pointed to the dazzling night sky, filled with glittering stars.

"See, Tande," she said to the baby, using the same words her mother had said to her long before, "those stars are watching over you. They will protect you all of your life. We have nothing to fear."

But soon the baby grew, as hungry babies will, into a child too big to carry on a mother's back. He crawled along Themba's clean, polished floor for a time, and then he pulled himself up and began to walk, tentatively at first and then with confidence. He quickly learned how to open the thatch door of Themba's hut and join the other naked children in outdoor play in the sunshine. In time, he could run faster than Themba. He giggled at her failed efforts to catch up with him. He became a boy.

One afternoon in late 1888, when a new, young missionary came to call on the kraal, he thought he saw from the corner of his eye as he hitched his horse to a spindly tree outside the kraal's narrow entryway, a group of little children frolicking in the interior. And among them, he thought he saw, was a white child, bronzed by the sun, with long fair hair — a little girl, he thought, maybe four years old.

He blinked his eyes, removed his spectacles and cleaned them with his handkerchief. *So much dust and dirt in Africa. Too much sun and heat,* he thought. He mopped his wet brow and the sides of his sweaty face. He was hot in his black suit and hat, but he had to keep up appearances. He had to be a model of civility and decency. To go around naked, or even half-clothed as these Zulus did, was indecent in God's eyes.

But there were times, moments like these, when he felt the sun was getting to him and he wished he were back in cool New England. He'd actually imagined that he'd seen a white child at play in a Zulu kraal! He shook his head, replaced his glasses and took another good look. The children had disappeared. He must have been seeing things. *Africa is so strange, he thought. Why on earth has God sent me, of all people, here?*

The young missionary strode into the kraal hurriedly, alarming the meandering goats and chickens in his path. He greeted the people he passed — the very old and the very young who were exempt from hunting or working in their fields — loudly in Zulu, startling the old people snoozing in the shade.

"Where is your chief?" the young white man demanded of an old woman in his newly acquired language.

"He is resting in his hut," she said, pointing to the largest, most ornate hut farthest from the kraal's entrance.

As the missionary headed there, the woman warned, "but he does not like to be disturbed from his naps." Unfortunately, the young man could not decipher her words; he had not yet learned the Zulu verb for "disturb."

Amma, too far along in her first pregnancy to work in the field now, intercepted the young man's approach to her father's hut.

"My father sleeps," she said to the man in English, which took him aback.

"You've attended a mission school?" he asked her.

"No." She shook her head. "I learn." She motioned in the general direction of Avoca.

Assuming Amma's English was better than it was, the missionary explained, hurriedly, in his own, comfortable native tongue, that he had many more villages to visit that afternoon before returning to his mission station by nightfall. He needed to speak with this chief, briefly, right away. He pulled out his pocket watch and tapped its face.

Amma could not understand his words, which came tumbling out of his mouth like water rushing over a rocky stream after heavy summer rains. But she remembered the pocket watch mister had shown her years before.

"See, Amma," William had said, showing her how the watch's hands moved. "It measures time." He had tried to teach her about time.

Reluctantly, Amma approached her father's hut and called to him from the door.

"Father," she said in Zulu, "a white man is here to see you. He needs to speak with you now-now."

While Amma and the missionary waited for some time for the chief to emerge from his hut, the two sat silently together on low wooden stools in the shade. The missionary averted his eyes from Amma's swollen breasts and protruding belly. When the chief at last appeared, growling like a huge black bear rising from hibernation, the missionary stood up, bowed to the great man, and introduced himself in faltering Zulu:

"Sir, I am Edward Smith of the American Zulu Mission at Umsunduzi. We have opened a new school there for native children, and I would like to invite the boys and girls of your kraal to come to our school."

The chief said nothing in response. Instead, he studied this ghost-man dressed all in black — analyzing his face, his eyes, the movement of his hands, and the

sound of his voice to determine his true motives. Was
he looking for Themba's Tande? Had he spied the ghost-
child? Did he plan to take the child away? Would this
child bring bad luck to his kraal after all?

Frustrated by the chief's silence, the missionary
turned to Amma and spoke in English.

"Tell him I'm a missionary of the Gospel," he said
to her. "The Gospel is the good news of God's love. God
is Love!"

His words, again, tumbled out too rapidly for
Amma to understand. But she did grasp, she thought,
the last line: God is Love. Themba had named her
ghost-child Tande, meaning Love. She hesitated at first
to translate for her father. Finally, she told him flatly, in
Zulu, "This man says that Great-Great is Tande."

At this, the chief bellowed as if struck by a spear.
"NO!" he thundered. "This cannot be!" He threw up
his heavily braceleted arms and stormed back into his
hut. Amma, fearful of her father's rages and worried at
the thought of what he might do next, looked terrified.
The timid young missionary turned from her and left
hurriedly.

All the way back to the mission station, astride his tired
bay, Edward Smith wrestled with God. *Why, Lord,* he
cried in his heart, *did you send me here? This is not the
place for me! I belong in a church school in New England,
where the leaves turn red and gold in the brisk autumn
air, and there are clean, broad, tree-lined streets and quiet,*

book-filled libraries that smell of old paper and leather bindings.

The young missionary failed to notice the pink and purple pastel ribbons in the sunset sky or the swooping, crooning birds passing him by, or the delicate outline of the m'ssassa trees on the horizon. Instead, he only looked downward at the ground in front of his horse, fearing venomous snakes might suddenly spring from the tall grass on either side of the rutted path and cause his horse to bolt. He had heard African servants at the mission station speak of snakes they called *imambas,* which were known to approach from the grass, elevate, and throw themselves forward, sometimes even pursuing a horseman along the road.

As his horse clomped ahead, Edward thought of the Old Testament story of Jonah wrangling with God over God's mission for him in Nineveh. *I answered your call, Lord,* the young missionary argued. *I didn't run off in another direction, as Jonah did! Why do I feel as if I've been cast into the belly of a whale? Dear God, give me a sign! Show me a gourd, as you did Jonah.*

After a welcomed bath and a simple dinner with the others in the mission's communal dining room, at which he did his best to keep up appearances, smiling, nodding, and making small talk with his fellow missionary-teachers, Edward and his young wife Emily retired to their bedroom early. As she sat quietly at her dressing table, removing hairpins and carefully brushing out her long, straight, brown hair, Edward paced the room.

"Em," he said finally, combing his thick hair with his right hand and studying the floorboards, "do you think it's possible for God to make a mistake?" She watched his reflection in the mirror above her dressing table as she continued to slowly brush the ends of her hair over her thin, childlike chest. "Or do you think we might have made a mistake in thinking God wanted us to come here?"

Although they'd been married only six months and serving in Natal for three of those months, Emily knew her husband and his moods well enough to know not to respond right away. She bit her bottom lip and repeated to herself the first verses of I Corinthians chapter 13: *... Love is patient and kind ... it is not puffed up ... it seeketh not her own ... it thinketh no evil...* It would be best, Emily knew, to simply allow her high-strung husband to speak his mind for a while.

"Shouldn't God have known I would hate the heat and dirt and dust and insects and diseases in this god-forsaken place? Why, I almost died of that malaria last month! I survived, yes, but I'm sure it damaged parts of my brain." He paused and looked at her, anxiety etched on his bookish face. "Em, I feel as if I'm losing my mind. I fear I'm becoming delusional!"

He slumped onto the edge of their four-poster bed, which was draped with mosquito netting, and sunk his head into his cupped hands. Emily got up, sat beside him, and gently stroked his back.

"Just today," he said, "I thought I saw a white child with golden hair playing like an African with other African children in a Zulu kraal. And then the chief became angry and sent me away as if he were hiding something. … Or maybe I'm just imagining things!" He gripped his head tighter with both hands.

"We must pray," Emily said, gently guiding her husband to his knees by the bed, where she knelt beside him and led their entreaties to God for His loving guidance and tender mercies.

A few days later, while Edward was finishing his breakfast in the dining room with the others, Emily arranged for the two of them to take a fresh horse and a two-seater buggy out for the day. "I think I need a change of scene," she said to Edward by way of explanation when he emerged onto the mission house's wide veranda and into the blazing morning sunshine. Since their arrival, Emily had spent most of her days studying the Zulu language and preparing the classrooms and supplies for the new native elementary school. Edward could understand her desire to get away for the day. He didn't argue.

In fact, Emily had lain awake for the past several nights as Edward slept restlessly beside her. She had thought, she had prayed, and she'd come up with a plan.

This time it was her turn to speak. After they'd boarded the buggy and settled themselves in, she announced, "I would like to see about the possibility of that white child for myself, Edward. Please take me to that kraal. I know it is God's will that we should go there." Although his wife was as small as a not-yet-fully-grown girl and seemingly physically fragile, and although she always spoke softly and deferred to her husband on most matters, as a good Christian wife should, her carefully chosen words that morning were incontestable. Edward humbly obeyed.

Emily sat erect in her seat, hands folded in her lap, beside Edward, who snapped the reins repeatedly to make the horse move faster. The circuitous route back to the kraal would take at least an hour. It would take less time, he knew, if the path had been straight, but Africans, he'd been told, didn't think this way. It was their belief that evil travels in straight lines.

Their winding path swept over undulating hills, broad valleys, and narrow streams; stretches of green grasses and wild flowers, and numerous clusters of trees. Emily, like a vigilant bird, took it all in. She breathed deeply and exhaled with a sigh. "Beautiful countryside," she said.

Edward only sniffed, then chided the horse to "move along now."

"Nice breeze," she said.

Edward wiped his brow with his sleeve. "It's too hot."

"Sometimes, Edward," she proceeded slowly, "God puts us in uncomfortable situations to test us and teach us. Imagine how uncomfortable John Newton felt when his ship was so severely battered by a storm that he was certain he was about to die."

Emily began to hum then sing her favorite hymn, as though singing to the grassy expanse of the open veldt.

"...Thro' many dangers, toils, and snares, I have already come! 'Tis grace hath brought me safe thus far, and grace will lead me home!..."

There was no need for Emily to remind him of the story. Edward knew it well. When John Newton, author of the immortal hymn "Amazing Grace," was a young man he'd been a profane, profligate sailor on a British slave ship. Although he had tempted fate many times before, when that terrible storm arose and he saw his end might be near, he realized he'd be damned to hell for eternity for the part he'd played in the slave trade if the ship capsized and he drowned. In an instant, he turned to God, begged for mercy, asked for salvation, lived to become an ordained minister, and died of old age. "Amazing Grace" became his spiritual autobiography in verse.

Edward neither spoke nor sang. His face was clenched, his hands held tight to the reins.

"God doesn't make mistakes, my darling," Emily said at last, looking up at her husband lovingly. "He is the one and only perfect teacher."

Amma recognized the young missionary right away. She feared what her father might do if he came face to face with this white man again. Her father had been unwell and irritable lately, and she alone cared for him while most of the others worked in the fields. She knew it fell to her as a favored daughter to do her father's bidding and listen to his complaints. He complained he couldn't sleep. He claimed the ancestors were coming to him with warnings in the night; they spoke to him through bad dreams.

"What kind of dreams, Father?" Amma had asked him.

"Ghosts come to our village and take one of my children away."

Now the sight of this missionary — and the white woman with him — made Amma sick with worry.

Unlike her hurried husband, Emily moved slowly through the kraal, greeting the elders she passed in perfect Zulu and respectful deference. She smiled into the old women's faces; she admired their basketwork; she made soft clucking sounds of approval, which made the women smile back at her. When she caught up with Edward by the chief's hut at the farthest end, Emily saw him speaking with a beautiful young Zulu woman with a newborn baby strapped to her back.

"Emily, this is Amma, one of the chief's many daughters. She speaks some English."

"So happy to meet you," Emily said in English. Hesitantly, the two women clasped hands.

"My father sleeps," Amma lied. She tilted her head and closed her eyes.

Edward looked at his pocket watch and saw it was only mid-morning.

"We'll wait for him to get up," he said and looked around the chief's hut for a place in the shade where they could sit. Everything he saw looked to him to be dirty and chaotic — countless cackling, scrawny chickens scratching madly in the dusty earth; mangy, whimpering puppies, toddling drunkenly, searching for their emaciated mother and her engorged teats; braying goats wandering listlessly and leaving mounds of malodorous pellet-size droppings in their wake; discarded broken earthen pots and old, broken baskets strewn here and there. *How can people live like this?* Edward thought, not for the first time.

Amma didn't know how to tell them, in English or in Zulu, that her father had refused to see them at all. He would not emerge from his hut, he had said to her when she announced their arrival, until they had left his kraal. He had nothing to say to them; so silence, he felt, was his most honorable and peaceful tactic.

Amma found two low wooden stools for the couple and placed them side-by-side on the west side of the chief's hut, in its cool shadow. "Sit," she said in English.

Then she left them and came back with a gourd filled with fresh, clear water from the nearby stream. "Water?" she said, extending her arms as if the water-filled gourd was a sacred offering.

Suddenly, Edward was riveted. He reached out for the gourd with both hands. "Yes, please," he said, then offered the gourd to his wife so she could drink first.

Time passed, and still there was no sign of the chief. Every half hour Edward checked his watch. It was nearly noon, and his stomach growled. The merciless sun, now directly overhead, offered no shadows, no escape. He could hear little children playing in a near-by hut, but he saw nothing of interest. He dabbed his perspiring brow with his handkerchief. He thanked God for broad-brimmed hats.

Then Emily, who had been sitting patiently beside him, hands folded serenely in her lap, reminding him periodically that "patience is a virtue," poked his ribs. "Look," she said softly, nodding to the left. A stream of naked little African children, led by a golden-brown boy of about four with long corn-silk hair, marched single-file out of one hut and into another, heads high, chests out, brandishing imaginary assegais and shields, as if playing Zulu warrior games. Then the couple saw an albino woman, wrapped in a white shawl like a ghost, scurry into the children's hut and shut its door tight.

Edward's eyes widened in near-disbelief. "Did you see that?" he whispered to his wife. She nodded slowly. "What should we do?" he said.

In low tones, so as not to be heard and understood by Amma, Edward and Emily discussed their options: Take the child back to the mission with them? Try to find his parents somehow? Perhaps adopt him, if that search proved fruitless? They wanted to start a family — but adopt a four-year-old child who behaved like a savage? Out of the question.

"We must go now," Edward said to Amma when she returned with more water. "Please tell the chief we are sorry we could not see him today."

As Edward led his wife back to the buggy and helped her into her seat, he felt strangely elated, vindicated. He wasn't losing his mind after all. And God had given him a sign — the gourd he had prayed for. Yes! "I once was blind but now I see!" Amazing grace, indeed!

Approaching the mission station, Edward admired the orderliness of it all: the carefully tended fruit and vegetable gardens, the groves of lemon, orange, guava and mango trees, the lush banana trees and neat rows of spiky pineapple plants. An avenue lined by tall china trees led from the mission house to the chapel, and near the chapel was a triangular piece of ground they all called "God's acre," with its sacred cedar and oleander trees. Edward saw it all as if for the first time and thanked God for a renewed sense of mission, to bring not only the Gospel but also order and civility like this to the heathen.

Emily, shaken by the events of the morning, said nothing for most of their return trip. "We must report this child to the authorities," was all she could say when they finally reached the mission station.

London, 1889

Jamie Barrie kept to his resolve. He dealt with the death of his childhood friend Helen by burying himself alive. He worked himself to exhaustion on articles, book reviews, theater reviews, stories, novels and plays. Early on, he had promised his mother back in Kirriemuir that he would "make her proud" in his pursuit of a literary career in London. But now he had Helen in mind as well. He wanted Helen, wherever her spirit had gone, to look on him with even more approval and pride than she had had when she was alive on earth.

In fact, he developed the habit of imagining that Helen was actually sitting across from him at his writing table in his London lodgings while he read aloud, as he had always read aloud to his mother in Kirriemuir, whatever he had just written. His imagination, ever-overactive, now provided him with solace. He pictured Helen intently listening to his every word, to the very end.

Did you like it? he'd quiz her. *Did it ring true? Was there enough detail? Too few descriptions?* "My mother doesn't care for scenery — that's why there is so little of it in my writing," he explained aloud to Helen's spirit. He found that imagining Helen's presence not only became the antidote to his guilt and sorrow over her death, it also spurred him on in his literary climb.

He wrote authoritatively on a wide range of subjects, spending pleasant, quiet hours in London's reference libraries, as well as at a favorite bookshop, Denny's, on Holywell Street, a shabby, narrow alley that smelled to Jamie deliciously of old books. He filled his pocket-size notebooks with ideas and never wasted any of them. As soon as he finished writing one item, he'd begin work on another. Often, he'd work on several concurrently.

His writing, his sole passion, possessed him. He worked as if driven by a ghost — *Was it Helen's,* he wondered? — puffing on his pipe, pacing up and down his room, then returning to his writing table again to cover page after page with his small, almost illegible script.

When he'd first arrived in London, Jamie had set three goals for himself: to earn a pound a day, to reach some little niche in literature, and to become a favorite of the ladies. With his tireless industry and seemingly limitless talent, he succeeded at reaching his first two goals, beyond his imaginings, within only a few years. But as a sorely shy man of only five feet tall, with stooped shoulders, deep-set eyes and forgettable looks, he found his third goal ever beyond his reach. He felt, he'd confided in a letter to Helen the year before, "a profound dejection about his want of allure."

Only Helen, among the women in his life who were not family, had accepted him for who and what he was, he felt. Only she had appreciated his idiosyncrasies and admired his creative talents. Once, he recalled, she'd even called him a genius.

Upon her death, then, Helen achieved a kind of sainthood in Jamie's mind. He placed her on a lofty pedestal, near those of his mother and sisters, against which no other woman could humanly measure up. In his dramatic imagination, Helen, his first leading lady, the star of all his childhood theatrical productions, became his ideal.

It was inevitable that Jamie's work also drew him to the London theatre. He now wrote theatre reviews not only for London's *St. James's Gazette* but also for Edinburgh's *Evening Dispatch* and other papers. Jamie attended these productions with his good friend Thomas Gilmour, known as T.L., an aspiring writer himself, who became Barrie's private banker because Jamie had no time for nor interest in his own finances.

The two men received press tickets to sit in the stalls, where Jamie would frequently fall in love — from afar — with a beautiful young actress. But he could never work up the courage to meet the actress in person. Instead, after the performance Jamie and T. L. would return to Gilmour's rooms to discuss the play — agreeing and disagreeing in good-natured companionship.

Jamie's literary ambitions had also led him, inevitably, to begin writing novels. His first effort, titled *Better Dead,* published at his own expense, lost him money. But by this time, Jamie could afford to lose some money; he was earning close to £1,000 a year from his other writing. He chose to continue living simply in London, but he generously sent sums home to his mother in Kirriemuir, ever intent on making Margaret Ogilvy proud.

She sent him grateful letters in response. "Do you remember when you were but a bairn," she wrote in one, "you used to say, 'Wait till I'm a man, Mother, you'll never have a reason to need!' and when I laid on hard beds, you said, 'When I'm a man you'll lie on feathers'?" Her letter continued, "Well, now it has all come true like a dream."

After having lived in London only five years, Jamie Barrie had published five novels, two of which focused on his hometown of Kirriemuir (disguised as "Thrums" in his fictional accounts) — *Auld Licht Idylls* and *A Window in Thrums.* Some of the reviews for his books were effusive, full of superlatives. One critic said Barrie wrote "extremely well," his narrative powers were "beautifully attractive in a clean, telling prose."

But some critics, especially his Scottish readers, were offended by Barrie's depiction of rural Scottish life in his Thrums novels. Acid criticism came from reviewers, schoolmen and other professional men who accused Barrie of "selling to the world a saccharine conception of the Scot all the more damaging because of the half-truths in it." In Kirriemuir itself, friends and acquaintances of the Barries did not hide their disapproval of Jamie's putting their stories into books that seemed to make fun of them.

Jamie, whose self-confidence and complete faith in his own star were rapidly rising, paid little attention to his critics. He kept writing. And he continued to read aloud his final drafts to Helen's spirit in the privacy of his room to gain her imagined approval.

Helen also became the inspiration for some of the women who appeared in his novels, such as Bell in the *Auld Licht Idylls.* This Bell was young, beautiful, and pursued by many suitors. She was "proud but modest," "brave, as well as energetic," he wrote. To illustrate this Bell's bravery, Barrie fictionalized a thief breaking into Bell's family's cottage one night when she was alone at home. Instead of running in fear, Bell stood up to the thief, telling him he ought to be ashamed of himself and not letting him out by the door until he had taken off his boots so as not to soil the carpet.

"Aye, this is so like you, Helen!" Jamie said, slapping his writing table with self-satisfaction. *"I'll immortalize you yet!"*

He wrote, as well, in another of his books of an unnamed "Heroine" whom he described as "a tall, majestic woman," eighteen years of age "and of remarkable beauty." Margaret Ogilvy, always assuming that all of the women in all of her son Jamie's books were based on her alone, questioned the identity of this heroine.

On one of his visits to Kirriemuir, while Jamie was reading this story aloud at the foot of his mother's bed, his mother corrected him.

"I was never tall — nor a beauty at eighteen," his mother said.

"Perhaps this story isn't about you this time, Mother," Jamie answered her.

His frail seventy-year-old mother only laughed. Turning to her daughter Jane Ann, she said, "He tries to keep me out of his stories, but he canna; it's more than he can do!"

Often these readings, meant to entertain, had to end abruptly because Margaret Ogilvy's mirth turned to violent fits of coughing.

Jamie's visits to Kirrie grew more infrequent. He was busy in London, where his work never let up and his social life improved. He was becoming known, admired, and invited to literary gatherings. In Kirrie, on the other hand, he felt the townspeople's scorn because of his Thrums books. And, too, he was haunted by his achingly intense memories of Helen and saddened by the news of her family.

His sister Jane Ann reported bits and pieces of this news to Jamie when they were alone in their parents' parlor at Strath View.

On one visit he learned that soon after Helen's death, her brother Davey joined the British army, where he served in Upper Burma during the Third Anglo-Burmese War. He had not returned home since.

Later Jamie learned that William's father John Black had died. "Of pneumonia, they say," Jane Ann said, "but others say of a broken heart."

On another, later, visit, Jane Ann told him that Helen's father Sandy David had abandoned his wife Agnes for a younger woman. "People say that he and the hussy are 'livin' in sin' in Dundee," Jane Ann whispered.

Jamie said nothing.

"Agnes is doin' poorly, poor soul," his sister added.

Jamie knew he should visit Agnes, pay his respects, and try to cheer her in some small way. But what could he say? What would make it right? He knew he would become tongue-tied. She would weep and he would freeze, unable to reach out and touch her old, soft, bent body. He envisioned the visit clearly. It could only go badly. He would fail at comforting her. He would be a failure. His guilt and sorrow would overwhelm him. She would see it in his eyes. He could not face her.

All he could do, he felt, was ask his kind-hearted older sister Jane Ann to pay a neighborly visit to Agnes in his stead and give her his sincerest regards, as well as a small sum of money on a regular basis. He could afford to do this much.

Zululand, 1889

Melmoth Osborn had better things to do than to lose
sleep over one small boy, even a white boy. Osborn's primary responsibility, as he saw it, since his appointment
as the first Resident Commissioner and Chief Magistrate
for the newly annexed Zululand in May 1887, was to
secure the peace and safety of the region and its people.
At fifty-three, he was tired, tired of the wars and blood-
shed, tired of the complications and miscommunica-
tions, tired of trouble. All he really wanted was peace.

Osborn had spent his entire adult life in this
mysterious part of the world, and he loved it still, for
reasons he had to remind himself daily. Yes, he had to
admit, he was still in love with its earthy beauty, its rolling hills and stretches of green grassland, its flat-topped
mountains and the waterfalls that fell like bridal veils
out of nowhere. He still loved riding into the countryside and breathing its sweet air, spiced with the woody
fragrance of cook fires from Zulu kraals. The majestic beauty of Zululand's raw nature always succeeded
in restoring, at least to some extent, his weary soul. He

also understood this land and its people better than almost any other British administrator of the day. He prided himself on speaking fluent Zulu and getting on well with the natives. The Zulus called him *Nobuhlobo:* Friendly.

In fact, he had a deep, unspoken respect for the Zulu nation, in, as he would put it, "all their superstitious madness and bloodstained grandeur." As a young man of twenty-two in 1856, he had witnessed with his own eyes at close range the grim, historic battle between the rival Zulu princes, brothers Cetewayo and Umbelazi. With the temerity of a young man, Osborn had swum with his horse across the Tugela River before dawn and hid in a wooded area in the middle of the battlefield, hooding his horse's head with his coat to keep the animal from neighing and thus giving his position away.

When the two opposing sides met — both many thousands of warriors strong — the earth literally trembled, and the roll of their shields as they came together "sounded like heavy thunder," Osborn later recalled. In this one battle, tens of thousands of Zulus perished, and the young Osborn only just escaped with his own life — by riding back to the Tugela at nightfall and swimming with his horse across the river's black, corpse-clogged waters.

From early on in his administrative career, Osborn had seen the Zulus' virtues as well as their vices. Yes, they were fierce, but they were also loyal, and they feared neither wounds nor doom. Yes, they could slay unsparingly, but they were never mean or vulgar. In Osborn's view, for these people, who continually faced the last great issues of life or death, "meanness and vulgarity were far removed."

The news, then, of a blond white child found in a Zulu kraal failed to alarm Zululand's Resident Commissioner the way it had alarmed the nervous American missionary, Edward Smith, who had come to report his recent find, excitedly describing the child as a savage. Osborn knew instinctively that the child was being well cared for by the Zulu mothers; the boy's life was not in danger. What did concern him, though, was how in heaven's name the child got there in the first place, and what effect this unsettling news would have on the British immigrant community.

He wished he could visit the kraal in question himself, straightaway, sit with the chief and listen, truly listen, over the course of, say, an afternoon, to the slow unfolding of the whole story, to get at the truth. But the Resident Commissioner had a report due to his superiors in London, a report on the status of things in Zululand, and he had to write it in a way that these men might understand.

Such reports never failed to cause Osborn anguish. How could he ever express in clipped, official, Oxford English the musicality of the Zulu language, the Zulus' metaphorical way of thinking, the raw beauty of their way of life? He felt like a failure before he even put pen to paper.

His mind cast back thirty years.

When he was still a young, adventurous bachelor, he had had a Zulu lover. One moonless night when he was visiting her kraal, as he was stroking the smooth, taught skin of her strong back and she was smoothing his soft, tussled hair in the darkness, she whispered in his ear in Zulu, "You can never know."

Know what? he'd thought then.

Ever since, he'd made it his personal mission to learn what she'd claimed he'd never know. But his regular reports to London, he felt, could not possibly convey the mysteries and intricacies he knew to be true of Zululand. English simply lacked the words.

What his superiors in London cared about, Osborn knew too well, were revenues and immigration. These two concerns went hand in hand. Prosperous colonies enriched the Empire, and able-bodied British subjects of childbearing age who emigrated to the colonies helped to make that prosperity possible. They became the "bosses" — the soldiers, the colonial government administrators, the gentlemen-farmers, the railway men, the businessmen and entrepreneurs, and the mining engineers who managed to extract all the riches that the colonies had to offer. In Africa, there was no end to cheap labor. And where that African labor had proved unreliable, such as in the sugar plantations outside of Durban, where the Zulus chose not to work, "coolies" by the thousands were imported from India to work as indentured servants.

Especially since the recent discovery of large gold deposits in the Transvaal, there had been a welcome influx of British immigrants and healthy investments. Now, the news of a white child being "stolen" by Zulus and raised "like a savage" would, Osborn feared, surely spread like a wild fire skittering across dry veldt on a hot and windy day. This devastating fire would send young, new immigrant couples scurrying back to the safety of "civilized" Britain, and in turn cause prospective British immigrants' adventurous dreams to die.

In an effort to keep this matter quiet, then, Osborn swore his deputy to secrecy. He commissioned him to travel alone, on horseback, to the kraal that the missionary had indicated on a map. He had to locate the child, talk with the chief, get the history, and bring the child back to Osborn's house in the Mthonjaneni district under cover of darkness. No one was to see him and the child return. No one, not even the deputy's wife, was to know. The young man, a devoted father of three whose facility with the Zulu language was sketchy, dutifully accepted this, his latest assignment, and set off immediately.

The chief couldn't sleep. No matter which wife he visited in the night, no matter what she did to soothe him, whether singing to him softly or rocking him gently in her ample arms, the chief's vivid dreams soon woke him, causing him to gasp as if struck with an assegai.

"What is it, my husband?" his second wife, Amma's mother, asked when he woke with a start one night.

"Are you ill, my husband? Is it your heart?"

He could not explain to her that the spirit, *umoya,* of his first wife, Themba's mother, had come to him in a dream. She was large and dark as a thundercloud, carrying a lightning bolt in her right hand like a spear. When she walked toward him, with fire in her eyes, the earth trembled then broke apart, causing his entire kraal and all of its people, men, women, and children, precious cattle, and all other animals to tumble into the deep fissure. As he, too, fell into this bottomless chasm, he heard the monstrous dream-woman scream, "My child! My child!"

The chief told his wife it was "nothing," patted her arm, and instructed her to go back to sleep. Then, for the remainder of the night, he stayed awake, thinking. Why was his first wife haunting him? What was she trying to tell him or warn him of? She had been a gentle woman in life; how had she become so ferocious in death? Should he summon an *inyanga?* No, he did not need a medicine man; he was not sick. Should he consult an *isangoma* to interpret his nightmares?

His head ached. So much had changed since the ghost people had come in and forced their laws upon his people, claiming this region as their Zululand. Now Zulu men of any age could marry, even before they "wet their spears" in war, as was the case before. And Zulu men could now leave their kraals and work for wages in Natal or the Transvaal, or elsewhere, as they wished. Zulu arms were now banned and intertribal wars were outlawed. He himself and all of the Zulu chiefs were now subjects of the British Resident Commissioner.

Fortunately, the chief had known for many years the man who had been made Resident Commissioner of Zululand, and he had come to trust him. Prior to the annexation, this Mr. Osborn had held meetings with the leaders of the Zulu nation in which he'd patiently listened to their views. Then, in turn, in clear, fluent Zulu, he conveyed to them the benefits of their being placed "under the protection and supreme authority of the British government." Mr. Osborn stressed the need for peace. The Zulu leaders asked for time to consider. But within months the decision was made by other chiefs, who lived far, far away, across the great seas, in that place called London.

In May 1887, without the consent of the Zulu leaders nor Osborn's official recommendation, Zululand became a British possession.

Dark thunderclouds rimmed the horizon like an advancing Zulu army as Osborn's deputy approached his destination. His heart thudded wildly in his chest. There was no telling what might happen when he confronted these Zulus, he thought. What if there was trouble? For reassurance, he patted his sidearm buckled in its holster beneath his coat. But what if he were overpowered and murdered on the spot? What would his wife and children do without him? He imagined that she would surely return to England and forever regret the day she ever agreed to emigrate with him to South Africa. His children would grow up without him; they would soon forget him. His mood became as gloomy as the darkening sky.

When he reached the kraal, the skies opened and the summer afternoon rain began to fall in torrents. He dismounted quickly, tied his horse to a tree, and shook the rivulets of rain from his hat and clothing in a futile effort to make himself appear more presentable. With a polite bow, he greeted an old man at the entryway to the kraal's circular outer stockade and asked to see the chief. In hesitant Zulu he told the man that he was an envoy of Melmoth Osborn, Resident Commissioner and Chief Magistrate for Zululand. He repeated the name Osborn twice so the man would be sure to grasp it.

With the barefoot old man leading the way, brown mud oozing between his brown toes, the deputy walked slowly to the far end of the kraal toward the chief's immense beehive-shaped hut. The rain had sent the people into their respective smaller domed huts for shelter, but the deputy could feel their eyes on him as his high leather boots squished in the old man's tracks. The cattle, gathered in the central circular pen, were restive, no doubt due to the thunderclaps that followed each distant bolt of lightning. The smaller, freer animals were in hiding.

When Amma saw the white man approach her father's hut, she hurried to intercede.

"Hello," she said to the man in English.

Surprised, he asked her in English whether he might see the chief.

As the three took cover from the downpour beneath a thatch overhang by the entrance to the chief's hut, the old man spoke rapidly in Zulu to Amma, repeating the name Osborn several times, followed by "*Nobuhlobo.*"

"I will speak to my father," Amma said, disappearing into the low doorway. And then within minutes she motioned that the deputy should come in.

To receive this government representative, the chief had donned his finest leopard skin cloak and a necklace with leopard claws. One tall feather rose up from his leopard headband. His thick arms and ankles were heavily braceleted in copper. His enormous feet were bare. Befitting his position, he sat on a large, carved, wooden throne-like chair with a high back and arm rests. At first glance, the chief appeared fearsome, but once the deputy's eyes adjusted to the dim interior light, he could see that the chief seemed harmless, exhausted, as if all the fight he may once have had in him when he was a young warrior had been depleted by time and countless circumstances far out of his control.

Speaking in sonorous Zulu and relying on Amma to translate where needed, the chief inquired as to Nobuhlobo's wellbeing and asked the reason for this envoy's visit.

"We have learned," the deputy said, choosing his Zulu words with care, "that you are harboring a white child here, and we would like to know how this came to be."

Knowing there was no escape now, the chief ordered Amma to call in Themba and the boy.

"You see," the chief said, when Themba arrived in the doorway, head bowed and squinting, clutching the naked boy by her side, "he is the child of my white daughter!"

Is this possible? the deputy wondered. *Can an albino woman give birth to a blond-haired, blue-eyed child whose skin is the color of gold?*

Although Themba trembled in fear, these words of her father warmed her heart. He had called her "his white daughter"; he had claimed her. He had said she was the mother of this boy, her Tande; he had honored her. For the first time in her life, she felt her father's love.

The deputy turned to Amma and spoke in English. "Is she the real mother, the birth mother of this child?"

Amma could not lie. "No," she said. She looked at Themba's colorless face, her pale, terrified eyes. This was the day they all had dreaded. But she had to tell the man the truth. "His blood mother and father died soon after he was born. My sister became his love mother."

In the next hours, in broken English and half-understood Zulu, the deputy learned the full story from Amma, while Themba and the boy sat silently side by side on low wooden stools on a far side of the room. The boy could sense the fatefulness of this meeting. He saw the terror in Themba's pale blue eyes. He felt her slim body shake uncontrollably beneath the once-white linen shawl she wore wrapped around her head and arms and shoulders like a shroud. He held her hand and tried to soothe her. It had been instilled in him already, even at this early age, that boys and men had to be strong like spears. Women could be soft, they could tremble in fear and weep openly, but men could never do so. So Themba's Tande resolved to be strong, like a warrior, for her.

"His blood mother was Helen," Amma said to the man, indicating to Themba that she needed to show him the shawl. "See?" She pointed to the blue embroidery, now faded and worn. "Helen David of Kirriemuir."

"I see," said the man, reaching for the shawl. He could barely take it all in. A young Scottish couple in Avoca murdered by drunken young men almost five years before? Their infant son rescued by the Zulu nanny? He'd never heard a word of this preposterous story, but then he'd only been in South Africa for three years. "Well," he said, getting to his feet, "I am under orders from Mr. Osborn to return this boy to his people. He must come with me."

With that, he bowed to the chief, thanking him for this audience and for his "cooperation with the crown in this matter." He then tucked the crumpled linen shawl under his arm, took the boy's hand and walked the distance to the kraal's entrance with feigned confidence, hoping that no one armed with a long spear would stand in their way. The little boy beside him walked with his head high and his chest out, pretending to be brave.

By this time the rain had stopped and the sinking sun was ablaze in the western sky. The deputy removed his coat and wrapped it around the naked boy, then lifted him gently onto his horse. He had a son about the same age, nearly five, whom he loved with his whole heart. So his heart went out to this silent, stoic, poor little orphan boy.

He mounted his horse, held the boy close with one arm, and slowly headed back to Osborn's house so that they would return after nightfall.

John

The boy had never been this high up before except in a tree but trees didn't have legs like this big horse and make noises that sound like KALUMPKAHLUMP-KALUMP. Trees swayed in strong winds sometimes and he fell from one once but trees don't move forward like this going... WHERE? ... *Where are we going?*

The horse made other noises too — snorting noises like the cattle made sometimes in their pen as if they were saying LET US GO FREE!

The man's arm around his middle felt strong and kind at the same time so he knew he wouldn't fall from the horse like he'd fallen from the tree. The man held him tightly to himself — the way Themba had wrapped him tightly to her body when he was small enough to fit on her back. But now he was big enough to ride on a horse, and the horse was going forward, away from all that he knew so he wanted to know. *Where are we going?*

The man tried to speak to the boy but the boy couldn't understand what the sounds he made meant so the man gave up and talked to the horse instead saying

GIDDYAP and slapping the switch connected to the horse's mouth with the hand that wasn't holding the boy around the middle. Then the horse snorted again and reared his head as if he were saying WOULD YOU RATHER WALK? The man didn't argue with the horse.

As soon as the sun went off to bed on the far side of the earth and the fat moon came out to play with all the bright stars dotting the black sky the boy knew everything would be all right because Themba had always told him the stars would watch over him.

"See, Tande," she always said, pointing to the night sky in the cool evenings when they were free to walk outside together, "those stars will protect you all of your life. And when I die I will hold a special star in my right hand like a fiery torch, which will guide you on your life path. You will never have anything to fear."

So the boy felt safe wrapped in the man's strong arm as the horse kahlumped along the moonlit path beneath the star-splattered sky.

The boy wasn't afraid because he was a Zulu warrior. But what he wanted to know, but was too shy to ask, was *Where are we going?*

KALUMPKAHLUMPKALUMP…

That big-mooned sky made the boy want to tell the man one of the many stories Themba had often told him — how Great-Great lived in a kraal behind the sky and when people died their spirits went to his kraal and they became his subjects and their work for him was to assist their descendants still alive on earth by listening to their supplications and sometimes — if they were very good people — answering their prayers.

But the man wasn't looking up at the sky at all — his eyes were on the silvery moonlit road ahead, hoping his horse wouldn't be spooked by the sudden appearance of any nocturnal animals. And, besides, the man would not have understood the Zulu words of the boy's story anyway.

So the boy kept his silence and stared at the sky, counting the stars until his eyes burned from the fiery brightness — all the while wondering, *Where are we going?*

Zululand, 1889

By the time the deputy reached the back door of Melmoth Osborn's sprawling thatched house, the boy was asleep, no doubt rocked to sleep by the horse's steady, swaying gait. *If only my son would fall asleep so readily,* the young man thought, as he covered the boy completely with his coat and carried him like an inert bundle up the back steps.

Osborn and his wife greeted the deputy quietly so as not to wake the sleeping boy. They directed him to a soft, old settee on the newly installed, wire-mesh, screened-in veranda, where the child would spend the night, watched over by their native houseboy, a diminutive Christian convert called Paul, who had been sworn to secrecy.

"You will guard him with your life, Paul," Osborn ordered the timid little man.

"Yes, boss," Paul responded with clenched hands and a low bow.

It was a cool, quiet night, and the boy slept soundly, even when his slight, golden-brown body was unwound from the deputy's coat and wrapped in clean, warm blankets. "What a beautiful boy he is," Mrs. Osborn remarked wistfully, noting the child's fine, pale, silken hair and his lean, muscular limbs. She and her husband had had no sons, only two daughters, now grown and married but as yet childless.

"What shall I find for him to wear?" she fretted. "We only have the girls' old clothes in trunks. Could he wear little girls' undergarments? He can't go around naked like this," she whispered.

Osborn shrugged. He had more pressing concerns. He had to learn the Zulus' story from his deputy. He had to determine who this child was, where he came from, and what could and should be done with him.

"You must be hungry," Mrs. Osborn said to the deputy. "Won't you stay for supper? I'll have Paul fix a place for you."

"Thank you, Madam, but I must be getting home soon. My wife will be worrying where I've gone off to."

"You're not going anywhere until you give me a full report," Osborn said, trying to seem gruff. "I've sent *my* bloody report off to London, now I'm ready to hear *yours.*"

While Paul sat like a sentry on an old wooden chair beside the sleeping boy and Mrs. Osborn searched through old wooden trunks for suitable children's clothes, Osborn and his deputy sat in his book-lined study overlooking the gardens and talked. In minute detail, the deputy told his superior the whole story that he'd learned that afternoon.

"A Scottish couple murdered by drunken young men in Avoca? Why, I never heard of such an incident! No, wait—" Osborn ran a weathered hand across the top of his balding head. "I seem to recall now that there was an accident in Avoca—a brush fire. The whole place burned down and the whole family with it."

"The chief's daughter tells it differently," the deputy insisted. "She was their nanny. The boy was only weeks old. When the three men arrived, drunk, with guns, looking for trouble, the mother told the nanny to take the baby to safety at her kraal. This nanny, Amma, heard the shots and the screams. She saw the fire." He paused. "The child has been cared for by Amma's sister, an albino, ever since. The boy thinks that she, the albino woman, is his mother."

"Preposterous, indeed!" Osborn interrupted.

"But I have proof. Amma gave me this—"

The deputy pulled from his leather knapsack Helen's linen shawl and handed it to Osborn. "See the embroidery in the corner? Amma claims the boy's mother wrapped him in her shawl before sending Amma and the child off. The albino has been wearing the shawl ever since."

"Hmmm," said Osborn, turning the shawl over in his hands, "Helen David of Kirriemuir. Kirriemuir's a little village in Angus, if I'm not mistaken." He stroked the fabric. "Good Scottish linen. Wears like iron." He brought the shawl to his nose, closed his eyes and breathed deeply. "Smells like wood smoke… like Africa." After a moment of reverie, Osborn turned his attention back to his deputy.

"Do you believe this story? Do you think this Amma is telling the truth?"

"I do, sir," the deputy said.

"Then this is what we must do…"

When the boy woke with the sun he thought he was still dreaming because nothing was familiar to him but when he felt his face and his hair and his arms and all around him these coverings and this soft bed everything he touched felt real to him but where was he now? And where had the horse gone?

When could he ride on the horse again?

He called out to Themba but she didn't hear him — she didn't come to him as she always had when he called her name — *WHY?*

Instead a small, dark man with dark eyes bent over him and said to him in Zulu, "There, there. All will be well. God will take care of you." He stroked the boy's smooth hair. "Are you hungry?"

The boy felt his stomach and realized it was empty and yes he was very hungry and thirsty too. The little man wasn't Themba but he understood the boy's needs and he spoke words the boy could understand so the boy nodded his head and the man smiled a broken-toothed smile at the boy and quickly brought him a warm bowl of mealie-meal porridge and a tumbler of fresh milk.

"All will be well," the little man said again. "God will take care of you." And then Paul began to sing a hymn with those words in it, while his head swayed in time with the music and he seemed to go into a swoon.

As the boy ate the porridge which tasted so much like Themba's porridge it made him feel at home he watched the man in wonderment having never seen such a man who was so much like a woman.

"Where is the horse?" the boy asked the man in Zulu. "When can I ride on the horse again and go back to my people?"

"You *will* be going back to your people," Paul assured him. "But not on a horse."

That day, the deputy followed Osborn's orders to investigate the accident, as well as find the boy's birth records and his parents' immigration documentation. *Who was this child? Where did he belong? What should he do with him?* These questions began to plague the Resident Commissioner and Chief Magistrate for Zululand, who was now guilty of hiding the child in his own home.

While the deputy investigated, Osborn and his wife conferred. She had long been begging him for a trip back to Britain, either with him if he could tear himself away from his work, or by herself. She had parents in the north of England, near the Scottish border, whom she hadn't seen in many years. They were getting old, she insisted; she needed to see them before they died.

Until now, Osborn's answer had been, "No, it's too far, and it's too costly."

He would tell her, "Not now, my dear," patting her hand.

But, he realized suddenly, that "now" had now come. His wife could be his accomplice. She could spirit this Zulu-raised child back to Scotland, to his relations in Kirriemuir, and no one here would be the wiser. No scandal. No fears. No mass exodus of young immigrant couples. His wife would get her wish to visit Britain, and the boy would be well cared for every step of the way.

"Yes, my dear," he said to her. "It's now time you saw your old mum and dad."

After the boy finished his porridge and his stomach felt warm and full, the timid little man took him outside to a place where he could bathe him with warm water and soap and dry him with a soft cloth and put clothing on him like the little man's. The feeling of the clothing on his skin made the boy want to itch the inside of his legs and the smell of the soap made his nose wrinkle up but the little man was gentle with him and sang the "God will take care of you" song in Zulu and then took him for a walk around the gardens and grounds.

The grass tickled the boy's bare feet. He saw no sign of huts or cattle. He saw no children and heard no laughter.

He was fascinated by the colorful birds with hooked beaks who complained loudly of being caged — SCREECH! LET ME OUT OF HERE!

If he were a bird instead of a boy he thought he would screech just like that and then he would find a way to break out of his cage and then he would fly back to Themba.

"Where is the horse?" he asked the man in Zulu. "I want to ride again on the big horse." He felt sure that if he continued to be a strong and brave boy he would soon be allowed to ride with the man on the big horse back to his kraal.

Osborn's deputy had done his job well. Sleuthing, he felt, could in fact become his professional specialty one day.

He'd remembered that Amma had said the boy's original, Christian name was John, and that she'd assisted in his birth at the couple's home. Perhaps this was why, the deputy thought, he could find no record of the boy's birth in the public records: The couple had not yet had time to register the baby nor baptize him in a church. So the deputy falsified a birth certificate, which would allow the boy to travel back to Britain and be placed in an institution if need be. He chose an arbitrary yet unusual date, some weeks before the "accident" took place, for the boy's birthday — February 29, 1885. No one bothered to question this "legal" document. No one stopped to realize that there was never a February 29th in 1885.

The deputy also made a point of reading all of the brief, faded newspaper accounts of the "accident" in Avoca. He learned that William had worked for the Natal Government Railways, so he made a trip to Durban to meet with the company's general manager, David Hunter. Hunter spoke highly of his young employee, as if he knew him personally. "Ach, wha' a terrrrrible trrrragedy!" the Scotsman said, shaking his head and rolling his r's with special emphasis.

"Did you ever suspect foul play in their deaths?" the deputy inquired.

"Why, no! Who would ever think of such a thing! Avoca is a peaceful little town. Our railway workers are safely housed and well looked after."

Opening the investigation, the deputy knew, would prove fruitless. Instead, he asked about the couple's family in Scotland. Hunter had his secretary dig into old files to find copies of the letters of condolence he had sent to William's father and Helen's parents in Kirriemuir. The deputy read these letters slowly, making a mental note of the recipients' names and addresses.

"Wha' is this all aboot?" Hunter said, leaning over his desk and looking at the young man over the top of his spectacles.

"Oh, it's just a routine inquiry, sir. We've had a report of an incident and we needed to follow up. You've satisfied my curiosity. Thank you for your time."

"Well, you know how those Zulus, are!" Hunter said with a laugh. "They can really make up stories!"

"Yes, sir. I know," the deputy said to be polite. And then he turned to leave.

Melmoth Osborn's next task for his deputy required him to return to the kraal with gifts of thanks: a copper bracelet for the chief, a beaded necklace for Amma, and a lovely, long piece of colorful fabric for Themba, to replace the linen shawl that had been taken from her.

"Tell them how much we appreciate their caring for the boy all these years," Osborn bellowed, as if his deputy were in a distant room and not sitting across from him, on the other side of his desk. "Tell them we know they saved this white child's life, and we are very grateful. Tell them we will be sending the boy back to his own tribe in Scotland across the great sea." Osborn gestured, making a broad arc with his arm, as if he himself were there at the kraal explaining to the Zulus the concept of this unfathomably far place on the other side of the world. "Tell them the boy will be well. Tell them that I, *Nobuhlobo,* will see to that."

"How will you see to that, sir?" the deputy asked softly.

"Well, I can't, can I. But tell them that. Just tell them. And tell them to keep it all quiet. This can't get out. Do you hear me?"

"Yes, sir," the young man said. "I hear you."

On the surface, life at the kraal had returned to normal. The people went about their daily tasks — able-bodied men caring for their cherished cattle, able-bodied women working in their fields, elderly people weaving reed baskets while watching the little ones close to home.

"The industriousness of these people," Osborn liked to tell his staff, "is impressive. Everyone works for the good of all. Even the infirm and feeble-minded have their place. No one is negated. We could learn something from them."

But, as the deputy was about to learn, there were exceptions.

When he arrived at the kraal, he learned that the chief was indisposed; he was too ill to see visitors. Amma spoke with the visitor in her father's stead and conveyed the chief's apologies to Nobuhlobo. She listened to the deputy's message from Nobuhlobo, and she accepted his gifts of thanks with a bow.

And Themba? When the deputy asked to see her and give her the cloth, he was met with a blank stare.

"Gone," Amma said, finally, in English.

"Where?" the young man said.

"Disappeared."

"How can that be? Did she die? Did someone kill her?"

Amma shook her head as if to say, I don't have the answers.

"The people say," Amma said at last, this time in Zulu, "that ghosts do not die. They just disappear. They believe that Themba and her Tande were ghosts, not real people. Both of them disappeared. Tande went off on a horse, and Themba walked into the veldt that same night and never came back."

"And no one sent out a search party to look for her?" the deputy said.

"Ghosts become invisible," she said. "They disappear."

"Well, then, here—" the deputy said, handing the cloth intended for Themba to her sister Amma. "You keep this."

The deputy never had occasion to visit this kraal again, but if he had done so the following year he would have seen Amma carrying a new baby on her back, wrapped in the colorful length of cloth he had given her. This healthy, robust, rich-dark-skinned baby would be a boy, and he would be named John.

Southmuir, 1889

Jane Ann Barrie read the brief telegram to Agnes in the privacy of the old woman's small cottage in Southmuir:

> Madam, your grandson John Black is alive and well. STOP. Sending him back to Britain. STOP. Can family take him in? STOP. Or shall we place him in state care? STOP. (Signed) Melmoth Osborn, Resident Commissioner and Chief Magistrate for Zululand, South Africa.

Jane Ann looked for a reaction from Helen's mother but found none. "Agnes?" Jane Ann asked, "Did you hear what I just read to you?"

The old woman, whose eyes had grown clouded, whose hearing had dimmed, and whose precarious health had declined dramatically since the news of Helen's death, sat impassively and stared directly ahead in the direction of the low window beside her loom. She didn't speak. Or even blink.

The truth was that Agnes, though she admitted this to no one, was nearly blind now. Oh, she could see colors, but there were no colors in her world. She could see objects, but their outlines were blurred. Like Queen Victoria, she dressed only in black; but unlike the queen, Agnes's view of life itself had grown totally dark. Her eyesight, and the reality of what she saw, pained her so much that she took to closing her eyes as she sat, wrapped in a thick woolen shawl by her hearth for most of the day. With closed eyes she could see again her two beautiful little children, playing beside her as she worked at her loom. And she could hear her bonny daughter's voice singing. Always singing.

Out of the kindness of her heart, Jane Ann had extended her caregiving duties in recent years to include the Barries' longtime neighbor, Agnes David. Jane Ann's goodness, as her brother Jamie often remarked, knew no bounds. "If there's a Heaven," Jamie liked to say, "my sister Jane Ann will one day be the Queen of it."

"Shall I read the telegram again, Agnes?" the young woman asked, leaning close to Agnes's better ear. "They've found Helen and William's child. He didn't die in the fire. They're asking, *Can you take him in?*"

Agnes turned her darkly clouded gaze toward Jane Ann. Tears slowly rolled down her ghostly pale, deeply wrinkled cheeks. *"How?"* the old woman said plaintively. *"How could I care for him when I canna' even care for mysel'?"*

The truth and poignancy of Agnes's words broke Jane Ann's heart. This news from South Africa, which would have brought joy to a tightly woven extended family, only brought more sorrow to Helen's bereft mother, whose husband and son had long abandoned her to a life of solitary grief and failing health. The tragedy of Helen and William's untimely deaths had torn the fabric of this small, fragile family to tatters. Will's father was dead, Agnes's son Davey was in a distant land serving in the army, and her husband Alexander had gone off wordlessly — this time, it appeared, forever — leaving no forwarding address.

How, indeed, could Agnes care for the boy? She knew too well her condition and her limitations. She could only hope that her only grandchild would grow and thrive in state care.

So, with a heavy heart, Jane Ann replied to Osborn's telegram on Agnes's behalf, expressing her deep regret that the family was not in a position to take the boy in.

John and Mrs. Osborn

The earth and everything on it — dirt, grass, trees, huts, cattle, goats, chickens, and even the big horse — have all disappeared! Everything has been swallowed whole by water — angry water that slaps against this ship and makes it rock. The water is everywhere all around as far as the boy's eyes can see. And everything he sees outside the round glass window is blue — blue water and blue sky — with white wisps of clouds up high and white foam frothing on the angry water below.

What is happening?

When he asks the nice lady in Themba's tongue, *What is happening? Where are we going?* she says softly, "I am taking you back to your country." But he cannot understand her words.

What is *"country"*?

He knows the nice lady is trying to be kind and good to him. She feeds him and bathes him and dresses him in clothes that will keep him warm now that the air outside stings. In the evenings she takes him for walks outside of their shared room so he can watch the stars.

She knows he feels better when he sees the stars. But he wonders why she ties a cord around him — as if he were a goat being led to the axe — to keep him from running away. She should know that he is too small to run away. Where could he go? And how would he get there? He cannot swim. Or fly.

Mrs. Osborn agonized. *If only Melmoth were here,* she thought. *He could communicate with this boy. He would know what to say and what to do with him. He always wanted a son. But, Lord knows, we are too old now to raise a small child. I must take him back now to where he belongs.*

I'm doing my best, but it's a frightful challenge. I only know a few words in the Zulu language, just enough to instruct servants: Cook this. Wash that. Change the bedding. Come here quickly.

At times I feel dreadfully deficient.

Yet, all in all, I must say, we're managing fairly well. I'm beginning to read the child's thoughts by studying his big, questioning, blue-green eyes. You might call it a mother's intuition. Yes, I've raised two daughters and have known many little ones in my day. But indeed I've never known another child quite like this one.

I've decided to make the most of this unique experience by making a study of him and keeping a journal of my findings. Who knows, it might be helpful to science. One hears of the odd white child being raised by Aborigines in Australia or by wild Indians in the American West. Well,

*this is a similar case, isn't it? Perhaps my findings will
be published and I'll make a name for myself, quite apart
from being Mrs. Melmoth Osborn, wife of the Resident
Commissioner and Chief Magistrate for Zululand. Perhaps
it's a good thing Melmoth isn't on this voyage after all.*

*Yes, I've resolved to see this as my new purpose, my
personal mission.*

*Let's begin with the physical observations: The boy
is well formed, of average height and weight, it seems to
me. He appears to be in good health, with bright eyes and
sound teeth; and he has a healthy appetite. When he first
came to us, a few weeks ago, he ate only mealie-meal, and
he ate it with his right hand. I have since taught him how
to use a knife, fork, and spoon; and he now eats whatever I
set before him, whatever I order to be sent to our room for
the two of us. Except fish. He indicated to me by shaking
his head vigorously and pointing to the plate that Zulus do
not eat fish. So I don't order fish for us anymore.*

*He sleeps well through the night, except for some
tossing and turning and whimpering in his sleep. Sometimes he calls out, "Themba!" but I try to soothe him in the
darkened room, and he falls back into a deep sleep. As he
sleeps he holds tightly to the tatty linen shawl he insists on
keeping, holding it close to his face as if he likes its awful,
muddy smell. How curious.*

*Intellectually, he appears to be quite bright and
inquisitive. I am teaching him English, little by little,
and he seems to be gradually acquiring a small but usable
vocabulary. Since we confine ourselves to this room (I fear*

he is not ready to be introduced to civilized society; he might just behave like a Zulu and embarrass me), I point to objects and provide him with their English names, and he repeats the words clearly and methodically: Bed, Pillow, Table, Chair, Book, Paper, Pencil. The next morning, when I quiz him on his newest words and I see he's remembered most of them, I smile and applaud. This makes him smile, shyly, too.

I've taught him "please" and "thank you" and a number of verbs, as well. We're making progress.

He is particularly interested in occupying his time with what for him must be complete novelties—paper and pencils. So I allow him to draw to his heart's delight. Mostly, he draws what he sees outside the porthole, the ocean waves and the cotton-wool clouds. Once, when we were in sight of another ship, he drew a semblance of that ship. He likes to draw birds in flight. He also copies pictures from books. He appears to have a natural talent for drawing! I only wish I had some of those new coloured wax crayons I've seen advertised for him to use here so he might colour his pictures in.

Emotionally, he is a stoic little lad. Like a miniature Zulu warrior, I sometimes think. He does not cry or fret or have tantrums of any kind. After all he's been through, it would be perfectly normal, one would imagine. But, no. He appears to hold his feelings tightly inside of himself. He stands stock-still while I bathe him and dress him, and he lets me put him to bed without any resistance. He does not fight me. His level of trust is surprisingly high. Perhaps it's

*just that he has a little boy's innate sense of wonder, and
this voyage is for him a great adventure.*

*It's only in his quizzical eyes that I sometimes read
some anxiety. His eyes seem to ask, "What is happening?
Where are we going?" I try to respond and reassure him,
but the questions in his eyes remain.*

*He is most calm at night, before bedtime, when I
take him out onto the empty deck for a brief walk while
everyone else is at dinner, and together we look up at the
stars. I confess, I must tether him because I fear he will
climb over the railing and be gone. What would I do then?
What would Melmoth think of me?*   .

*The boy is simply mesmerized by the starry nights. He
waves to the stars and calls to them in Zulu. I don't know
what he is saying, but it makes me happy to see him happy.*

*I'm growing fond of the little chap, and I like to think
he is growing fond of me as well. I am motherly, after all.
I'm sure he can sense that.*

The boy spots Themba's star. He knows it is hers because
it is the biggest and it has the most color. It is the color
of fire because it is a torch that she is holding up for him.
When he sees it his heart hears Themba singing *You are
my Tande, my gift. I will always love you and protect you.
I will light the way...*

He saw flying fish yesterday. They came up out of
the angry water and flapped their fins like wings for a
while then dove down into the sea again and were gone.
This is a true story. He saw them. The boy wished he

could be like them but he can neither swim nor fly. So he drew them instead.

For the duration of the voyage, Mrs. Osborn was alone with the boy and her thoughts. She had no one else to turn to on this unusual mission, so she talked to herself in her mind.

Melmoth would be proud of me. John Black is becoming a proper little gentleman under my private tute-lage. The people at the Dean Orphanage on Belford Road in Edinburgh will be impressed with the new boy I'm bringing to them, I'm sure. He is well behaved, quiet and obedient. He will prosper there under their guidance and care I have no doubt.

Good job Melmoth was able to arrange, in telegram exchanges, for the boy to live at the Dean. This institution's reputation is sterling. Magnificent housing — like a palatial stone mansion I'm told — designed by the renowned archi-tect Thomas Hamilton, Melmoth said; beautiful grounds for the children to play on; and excellent schooling, too, I hear. It's probably a blessing that the poor boy's old granny in Kirriemuir couldn't take him in. He'll amount to some-thing at the Dean. The boy has potential, and they will draw it out of him.

I've cut his long fair hair, so he looks more like a boy now. I couldn't bear to throw all of the cuttings away, so I saved a nice lock for myself in an envelope dated yesterday. Melmoth would call me sentimental, but I must hold onto something of this boy. Once I deliver him to the Dean and go on my way to visit my own old parents, I will likely never see this poor orphan John Black again. For the rest of my life I will wonder, How is he, really? And does he remember me and our time together on the steamship? I will then open this envelope, stroke the lock of his soft, honey-golden hair, and feel close to him.

The nice lady plays games. She teaches the boy songs and rhymes. *One two buckle my shoe three four knock at the door five six pick up sticks seven eight lay them straight...* When they go outside to look at the stars before bedtime, she sings a song about animals who were not swallowed up by the angry water:

> The Owl and the Pussy-cat went to sea
> In a beautiful pea green boat,
> They took some honey, and plenty of money,
> Wrapped up in a five-pound note.
> The Owl looked up to the stars above,
> And sang to a small guitar,
> 'O lovely Pussy! O Pussy my love,
> What a beautiful Pussy you are...'
> They dined on mince, and slices of quince,
> Which they ate with a runcible spoon;
> And hand in hand, on the edge of the sand,
> They danced by the light of the moon...

The nice lady is like a big child. She loves to laugh and play with the boy. He showed her how to march into battle like a warrior. They march around the room together, holding make-believe spears.

I've been thinking, Mrs. Osborn, who was always thinking, thought: *This has been a voyage of discovery for me as well. I now realize that I never spent this much concentrated time with my own children when they were John's age as I've been able to spend with him during these past weeks. In those days, when I was young and relatively new to life in South Africa, I did as other young mothers and left my little girls in the care of their African nanny while I went off and participated in "more important" activities, such as playing sports at the club in the mornings and having tea with my women friends in the afternoons.*

Ah, the colonial social whirl! So outnumbered by the Africans, we Europeans tend to huddle together in tight social circles, the way the Boers prepare for battle by arranging their wagons nose-to-tail in a circular, defensive laager. Meanwhile, while the young mothers are sipping tea, eating cakes, and gossiping, their little ones are sitting impassively in the shade of a distant tree with their ever-patient nannies. Why, I know British children whose first words were in Zulu!

I see now that children have much to teach us — even without a shared language — if we would only spend the time to learn from them. I'm grateful that Melmoth sent me on this mission. I know I will miss this little chap. I will always wonder whatever became of him. And I'll wonder, Does he remember me?

London, 1890

Jane Ann Barrie wasted no time in informing her brother Jamie in London of the news of Helen's boy: *He has been found! Alive and well! And he's been brought back to Britain and placed in a fine institution, the Dean Orphanage in Edinburgh.* "You must make a point of visiting him there at your earliest opportunity," she urged her brother time and again in her letters. And he tried his best to do so.

But other obligations — both professional and social — always intervened. Despite his best intentions — he did so want to meet the boy; he loved little boys and considered himself to be one still — he could not find the time. The appropriate time, like a wild bird in flight, evaded his grasp. And, though he would not likely admit this, he feared what such an emotional encounter with Helen's child would do to his equilibrium.

James Matthew Barrie, now thirty years old and living comfortably on Old Quebec Street near Marble Arch, was becoming an increasingly prosperous and famous writer. Everything he wrote, he sold. His latest novel, *The Little Minister,* also set in a fictionalized version of his hometown Kirriemuir, was selling well, boosting the sales of his previous Kirrie-based novels, *A Window in Thrums* and *Auld Licht Idylls.* He was working on a new play. And he continued to write serialized articles, which he sold without trouble, such as one called *An Edinburgh Eleven: Pen Portraits from College Life*—profiles of some of his college professors and others, including Barrie's literary hero Robert Louis Stevenson and his explorer-friend Joseph Thomson.

Barrie and Thomson, fellow-Scotsmen and friends from Edinburgh University days, had in fact recently spent six weeks together touring Europe—the Rhineland, the Tyrol, northern Italy, Switzerland, and France. During this trip, Barrie's first trip abroad, Thomson regaled his traveling companion with tales of his African explorations. Barrie had always enjoyed associating himself with men of action and adventure, and that passion had not diminished. Thomson was as much a hero to him at this stage of his life as he had been when they were in their early twenties.

Jamie never tired of the story of Thomson having been appointed geologist and naturalist to Alexander Keith Johnston's 1878 Royal Geographical Society expedition to establish a route from Dar es Salaam ("the harbor of peace") to Lake Nyasa and Lake Tanganyika in Africa. When Johnston suddenly died of dysentery and exhaustion on this expedition, Thomson, then just twenty-one, was left to take command, successfully

leading the effort over three thousand miles in fourteen
months and collecting countless specimens along the way.

"But they weren't all successes," Thomson admitted
to his friend Jamie on their European trip. "In Africa
dangers and disease are always lurking. I've been gored
by a buffalo, and I've suffered from malaria and dysentery more times than I can count. But it's been worth
it." Jamie's thoughts flew to his dear Helen. Was it worth
it for her? *No!* He turned his thoughts back to his friend
Thomson and never mentioned Helen's name.

Thomson repeatedly referred to the continent as
"my beloved Africa." His fondest boast was "not that I
have travelled over hundreds of miles hitherto untrod-
den by the foot of white man, but that I have been able
to do so as a Christian and a Scotchman, carrying everywhere goodwill and friendship, finding that a gentle word
was more potent than gunpowder, and that it was not
necessary, even in Central Africa, to sacrifice the lives
of men in order to throw light upon its dark corners."

Jamie was especially impressed by the Italian motto
that Thomson had made his own: *Chi va piano va sano,
Chi va sano va lontano* — "He who goes gently, goes safely; he who goes safely, goes far."

It was during this time in Jamie's life, too, that he
began receiving admiring letters from his hero Robert
Louis Stevenson, then living in Vailima, Samoa. United
in what he referred to as their mutual "Scotchness,"
Stevenson confided to Barrie: "It is a singular thing that
I should live here in the South Seas under conditions so

new and so striking and yet my imagination so continually inhabits that cold, old huddle of grey hills from which we come."

And in another letter to Barrie, Stevenson wrote of himself, "...I am a capable artist; but it begins to look to me as if you were a man of genius. Take care of yourself for my sake; it's a devilish hard thing for a man who writes so many novels as I do that I should get so few to read, and I can read yours, and I love them."

Stevenson's letters gave Barrie immeasurable pleasure. Barrie was becoming recognized, praised, and admired, not only in London, England, and Edinburgh, Scotland, but as far off as Vailima, Samoa, by a writer whom he idolized.

With all of his work, Barrie still made time for a social life. His mantelpiece was often lined with invitation cards. He was also, for the first time in his life, being noticed by women, who now regarded this formerly "strange, little man" as "amusing" and "charming." He relished the sea change. For him, the lower rungs of the ladder of success had been difficult to climb, but the upper rungs were getting much easier — and much more enjoyable.

The play that Barrie was writing, tentatively titled *The Houseboat,* had been in his mind for a long time, and he worked on it at every opportunity. It was set in a houseboat similar to the one he and his longtime friend T. L. Gilmour had once shared at Molesey on the Thames one summer. Barrie had so enjoyed that "gay and lively" summertime world — the boats and punts, straw hats, bustles and parasols, paper lanterns, laughter and leisure — that he sought to immortalize it in a play. This play was not the first he had written, of course, but he was determined to make this one his first theatrical success.

Letters from Jane Ann in Kirriemuir continued to arrive, inquiring of Jamie's plans to visit Scotland. "When you next come north," she nudged him gently, "perhaps you might stop in Edinburgh and see the boy at the Dean. Children have a way of growing up quickly, you know."

Each time, Jamie answered his saintly sister affirmatively: Yes, he had every intention of doing so, as soon as his work allowed; yes, he wanted to meet the boy and embrace him like family, and he would do so "soon." But the deeper truth was that Jamie was afraid. In recent years he had managed to successfully put his first leading lady, Helen David Black, out of his mind. He knew that seeing Helen's living, breathing child, face to face, would change all that.

Edinburgh, 1892

When his finished play, the title of which had been
changed to *Walker, London,* was being cast, Barrie
insisted that the role of the play's second leading lady
be a young woman who was very pretty; and he knew
just who should have the part. That person was the
twenty-nine-year-old English actress Mary Ansell, with
whom Barrie had been smitten some months before.
Others described her as "slim, quick-witted, determined,
and ambitious." Barrie admired, apart from her pretti-
ness, her pluck and self-reliance, her spiritedness and
her dexterity "in so many clever little ways."

Ansell got the part, playing the character Nannie
O'Brien to full houses every night. From time to time
Barrie dropped into the theatre and saw his second
leading lady looking prettier than ever. He feared he
was falling in love.

The only nagging worry that Jamie had was his
mother. Margaret Ogilvy's health had been declining
further, Jane Ann reported. And his own health had
been a worry for him as well. His chronic headaches

were getting worse, and his heavy smoking was causing him bronchial trouble. He didn't need Jane Ann to tell him he was working too hard.

Finally, in the spring of 1892, on his way from London to Scotland to see his ailing mother, Jamie became so ill he had to break up his journey and find a room in Edinburgh in which to rest and recuperate before he could continue north to Kirriemuir. Life, it appeared, was forcing him to meet Helen's boy, now seven years old. The Dean Orphanage was just a healthy walk from Jamie's hotel, and once he was rested enough to make the walk, he felt Fate pulling him in that direction.

It was a surprisingly warm Spring afternoon, and Jamie hoped that the stroll through Edinburgh's proud New Town, with its impressive squares, circuses, parks and terraces, would do him good, calm his overwrought mind, and soothe his sore lungs. The sky was unusually clear and blue — "the color of hope," as his mother would say — and the birds in the trees that lined New Town's streets were tweeting gaily. *Yes,* he thought, *this forced rest in Edinburgh was meant to be.* Long walks had always been one of his life's purest joys.

And then he saw it — with its vast stretch of verdant, perfectly manicured lawn surrounding the front — the immense, three-story, Craigleith-stone, neoclassical, porticoed and Greek-columned mansion, built like a castle or fortress to last forever. The Dean Orphanage took Jamie's breath away. *Helen's boy must feel like a prince here, he imagined.*

Climbing the wide stone staircase leading to the front entrance winded him; so Jamie stopped in the vestibule to cough for a moment, then catch his breath. There, to the left of the front door, he read an exquisitely carved, marble plaque dedicated to an honored office-holder of the orphanage, long deceased:

Thomas Tod, Esquire
who filled the office of treasurer
from XIII August MDCCLXXXI
till his death, March XXXI, MDCCXCVI

Not more remarkable for his zeal and unremitting endeavours to extend the benefit of this valuable institution than for his condescension and tenderness towards the helpless objects of it; he was followed to his grave by more than one hundred of them, bewailing, with tears, the loss they had sustained as if again bereft of a parent.

Jamie's eyes rested on the welcomed words "unremitting endeavours," "valuable institution," "tenderness," "as if" this man were "a parent," and his heart was buoyed by the hope, for young John Black's sake, that the Dean Orphanage and its parent-figures had not changed since Tod's day.

"May I help you, sir?" a short, stout, officious woman, appearing out of nowhere, asked abruptly.

"I'm here to see a boy," Jamie stammered, stifling another cough.

"Your name?" she demanded. "And the reason for your visit?"

"My name," Jamie hesitated, neither wanting to call attention to himself and his fame nor tell a blatant lie, "is Barrie." He coughed, holding his handkerchief over his nose and mouth like a partial mask. "James," he added, then thought, *Yes!* "Barrie James. And the boy, I've just learned, is a distant relation from Kirriemuir. His name is John Black. He is seven."

"All right, Mr. James," the woman said briskly, "wait right here, please. The children are having their afternoon rest now, but I'll see what I can do for you."

The boy looked ghostly pale and frightfully thin standing at attention beside the stern woman. His short fair hair was badly cut and disheveled. He wore gray institutional clothing and scuffed shoes. He regarded his visitor quizzically, with what Jamie read as fear in his eyes.

"It's all right, John," the woman said with neither hostility nor tenderness. "This Mr. James would like to visit with you for a wee while. You two can go out onto the front lawn for an hour. I will keep an eye on both of you. And then I'll call you back in."

Those eyes! Jamie thought. *The boy has Helen's eyes... William's straight, fair hair and fine nose... Helen's bow mouth and strong chin. This child is the perfect blend of both of them!* Memories of his early years in Kirriemuir when he knew and loved Helen David as a child of about John's age flooded his heart and mind. He had to breathe slowly and deeply to keep from coughing again. He reached out his hand to the boy. "Well, hello John Black, I've been looking forward to meeting you."

"Hullo, sir," the boy said timidly, extending a thin shaking hand.

"It's a beautiful day! Let's find a nice spot on the grounds and chat, shall we?" With that, Jamie Barrie took the boy's hand in his and walked with him down the front stone staircase, embarking on what he hoped would become a new adventure for both of them. As they walked he introduced himself. "My name is James, but you can call me Uncle Jamie," he said.

The boy said nothing. He didn't understand what the word "uncle" meant.

As the two walked on silently, looking for a suitable place to sit down, Jamie pulled out his pocket watch to check the time.

"Do you like stories, John?" he asked, not waiting for a reply. "Well, I'm sure you do. All little boys like stories! So let's find a place we can call our Story Seat, where I can tell you some of my best stories. Do you like that idea?"

The boy looked up at the strange little man, not knowing how to answer. None of the adults at the Dean had ever asked his opinion of anything. And they didn't tell stories.

"Here!" Jamie said triumphantly. "This bench will do. It's in the sun, but I think a little Scottish sunshine would do both of us some good, don't you? Let's sit down here." He sat, then patted the space beside him. "Come, sit beside me," he said. He paused, feeling awkward and unsure of how to begin. The boy sat stiffly, staring straight ahead, looking worried. Since their time was short, Jamie charged ahead.

"How are you, John? Are they treating you well here?"

Without looking up at the man, the frightened boy made a tentative nod.

"I came to visit you because I knew your mother."

Themba? the boy thought. *This little man knew Themba?* How could that be?

"We grew up together. She was beautiful. You look quite like her."

And with that the boy observed that the strange man began to talk as though to himself alone or to the distant trees, as if he were swept away by memories.

"...Your mother was so picturesque that she was the last word of art.... She was as mysterious as night when it fell for the first time upon the earth.... She was the thing we call romance, which lives in the little hut beyond the blue haze of the pinewoods...."

The boy could not grasp anything the little man was saying.

Suddenly Jamie was seized by a fit of coughing and filled with shame for his self-indulgence. "Oh, excuse me, John," he sputtered between coughs. "I'm so sorry. I must have gotten carried away! Well, I promised you a story, didn't I?" He looked at his pocket watch again. "Yes! I must begin!"

James Barrie's hotel near the Princes Street Railway Station was only about four miles from the Dean Orphanage. *A healthy walk,* indeed, he thought, as he set out to visit Helen's son for the second time. He walked west, the length of majestic Princes Street in the shadow of Edinburgh Castle, built high on ancient volcanic rock. He then bore right onto Queensferry Street and left onto Belford Road, all the while thinking of his explorer-friend Joseph Thomson who'd trekked thousands of miles along formidable, uncharted terrain in Central Africa — completely on foot — often while suffering from malaria or dysentery, or both. *I can do this,* Jamie told himself. *All I'm suffering from is a cough.* Along the way he stopped at a stationers to select a small gift for the boy.

The previous day's one-hour visit at the Dean had not gone as well as Jamie had hoped, and he'd suffered a fitful night's sleep as a result. Coughing and tossing, he'd lain awake fearing that he'd failed in his efforts to employ his prodigious storytelling powers to cast a spell on the orphan John Black and charm the boy into liking him. In recent years James Barrie had become used to admiration and unused to failure. So, in an effort to find a better strategy for their next encounter, he spent the remaining night hours reviewing what had gone wrong the day before:

The boy had sat impassively while Jamie told him stories about fairies. "When the first baby laughed for the first time," Jamie began, "his laugh broke into a million pieces, and they all went skipping about. That was the beginning of fairies."

The boy had no reaction.

Did he not understand the words? Aren't all children captivated by fairies?

Jamie pressed on.

"It is frightfully difficult to know much about the fairies. Almost the only thing known for certain is that there are fairies wherever there are children. They can't resist following children, but you seldom see them, partly because they live in the daytime behind the railings, where you are not allowed to go, and also partly because they are so cunning."

Still no response. Did the orphanage bar talk of fairies? Nevertheless...

"When they think you are not looking they skip along pretty lively, but if you look and they fear there is no time to hide, they stand quite still, pretending to be flowers. Then, after you have passed without knowing that they were fairies, they rush home and tell their mothers they have had such an adventure!"

Although they'd been sitting side by side on the outdoor bench, their Story Seat, on that first visit, the two were oceans apart, Jamie realized in his sleeplessness. How could an orphan relate to the idea of fairies rushing home to tell their mothers? John Black had no mother and no home to rush home to. And when Jamie had told the boy that his mother Helen had played a beautiful fairy queen in one of his own childhood plays, the boy could only stare blankly at him, as if the man were speaking French.

I must do better tomorrow, Jamie told himself repeatedly in the long, dark night. *I must review all of my stories — and invent new ones — and tell them as if they were conjuring feats!*

He considered telling the boy one of his favorite stories about birds — that all children were once birds and that the reason there are bars on nursery windows is because very little people sometimes forget they no longer have wings and they try to fly away.

"Quite the prettiest sight," as he liked to tell it to his young nieces and nephews, "is when the babies stray from their nannies in the park and are seen feeding the birds" — he liked to act this part out — "first a bit to me and then a bit to you, and all the time such a jabbering and laughing from both sides. They are comparing notes and inquiring for old friends, and so on; but what they say I cannot determine, for when I approach they all fly away."

Perhaps he might enjoy this birds story, Jamie considered.

But he knew he shouldn't add the part about little white birds being those birds who never had a mother.

What must it be like not to have a mother? Jamie couldn't imagine it. His own mother Margaret Ogilvy had been the bedrock of his life, his fiercest fan, the woman on whom he patterned many of his early female characters, the reason for his burning ambition. Since childhood, especially after his older brother David's devastating death at age thirteen, Jamie's primary purpose in life had been to please his mother and make her proud. David had been his mother's favored son, everyone knew. From David's untimely death onward, little Jamie tried his mightiest to fill the void.

How much did the boy John Black know of his mother Helen? Did he know anything at all? Jamie wondered. *Would it be wrong of me to ask the child?*

Jamie's own memories of Helen rushed in and filled his darkened hotel room. For a moment he even felt her presence, ghostlike, at the far end of his bed, so he pleaded with her softly, "Tell me what to say to your boy, Helen. Help me to know what to do. Give me the right story. Give me the words."

It was another, rare, warm and sunny afternoon, so the two sat side by side on the same Story Seat in the sunshine as they had the day before. Hands clasped in his lap, the boy sat stock-still, staring at the iron bars on the orphanage's windows in the near distance.

"I have a little gift for you," Jamie said. As the boy looked up, Jamie pulled from his coat pocket a slim drawing pad and a small packet of Crayons. Remembering that William had had a talent for drawing, Jamie thought the boy might have inherited his father's gift. John's eyes widened. He opened the packet and gasped at the bright colors.

"You must like to draw," Jamie said, and the boy nodded shyly. "Would you draw me a picture of what you are thinking?"

Jamie sat quietly and watched the boy begin — at first tentatively and then with more confidence. He drew clouds in a blue sky and evergreen trees in the distance and something flying between the earth and the clouds. It wasn't a bird. It was a boy.

"Is that you?" Jamie asked, pointing his forefinger at the flying boy.

John nodded.

"Well, then, I have a new story for you," Jamie said excitedly. A story suddenly hatched in his vivid imagination, as though it had been incubating in the back of his mind for some time. "It's about a boy, maybe about your age, who can also fly. This boy is a 'Betwixt-and-Between' — only half human — and we don't really know his age because he's never had a birthday."

With this, Helen's boy looked up at the man. He, too, felt like a "betwixt-and-between," and he had not had a birthday in many years because his birth date, according to the orphanage's records, was so odd, February 29th. Suddenly, he was exceedingly interested in the story of this flying boy.

Seeing he now had a rapt audience, James Barrie,

consummate storyteller, continued spinning this new yarn: "Well, his age doesn't matter in the least. This boy is really always the same age. The reason he escaped from being a human with birthdays is that he flew out the window — because it had no bars — when he was seven days old."

John Black was captivated.

"Standing on the window ledge the boy could see trees far away, which were doubtless in Kensington Gardens — that's in London — and the moment he saw them he entirely forgot that he was a little baby in a nightgown, and away he flew, right over the houses to the Gardens. It is wonderful that he could fly without wings, but perhaps we could all fly if we were as dead-confident-sure of our capacity to do it as he was that evening."

Perhaps we all can fly? John thought. He hung onto the strange man's words.

"At first the boy found some difficulty in balancing himself on a branch, but presently he remembered, and then he fell asleep. He awoke long before morning, shivering, and saying to himself, 'I never was out in such a cold night.'"

At this, James Barrie the storyteller shivered an imaginary shiver and coughed a series of real coughs before continuing:

"To the boy's bewilderment he discovered there were crowds of fairies running this way and that, asking each other stoutly, 'Who is this human in the Gardens after lock-out time?' but he never thought for a moment that he was the human.

"Finally," Jamie pressed on, "despairing of the fairies, the boy resolved to consult the birds, but now he remembered that all of the birds had flown away when he arrived. Poor little boy! Every living thing was shunning him. He sat down and cried. But—and this is a blessing—he never lost faith in his power to fly. The moment you doubt whether you can fly, you cease forever to be able to do it. The reason birds can fly and we can't is simply that they have perfect faith, for to have faith is to have wings!"

John was enthralled. *To have faith is to have wings!* He wanted more.

"I'll have to think of more such adventures and write them all down for you," said Jamie, pleased with himself at last. He smiled at the boy, and the boy shyly smiled back. John quickly tucked the pad and Crayons into the front of his shirt when the matron called him in.

On the morning of his third day in Edinburgh, James Barrie was feeling considerably better—well enough, he thought, to continue on his way to Kirriemuir. His ailing mother, he knew, would be worried about his welfare. Hadn't he left London days ago? He mustn't cause his mother further worry.

The sky, too, was a familiar thick, gray blanket of clouds blocking the morning sun and threatening a long stretch of rain. Not a day for sitting outdoors with the boy on their Story Seat, he feared. But he needed to see John Black one more time before he left for Kirrie. So, gripping his closed umbrella like a walking stick, he set out again on foot for Belford Road, stopping along the way this time at a bookseller's on Princes Street.

"John has a cold," the stout little matron scolded Barrie when he entered the vestibule and asked to see the boy again. "And no thanks to you, Mr. James, sir! I shouldna let him out with you and your deathly cough. And look a' the sky — it's about to let loose. No, he canna' go out today."

With some gentle coaxing Jamie managed to talk the woman into letting him see John, briefly, in the vestibule. "I'm leaving on the train for Kirriemuir this afternoon," he said, "and I need to say a proper good-bye." Jamie cocked his head pleadingly and affected his most winning smile. "Please, madam."

"Only a few minutes, then," she said. After a short wait, the woman brought the sickly child and left the two together.

Reaching into his coat, Jamie pulled out a small wrapped package.

"I have something very special for you today, John," he said, extending the gift to the boy. It's a book I thought you would like."

John's eyes widened. "Is it about the boy who could fly?" he asked breathlessly. This was the first full sentence Jamie had heard the boy speak.

"No, I haven't written about him yet. Those stories are still in here." He tapped his right temple with his right forefinger. "This is about another boy, Jim Hawkins, who finds a map that leads him to a place called Treasure Island." He removed the gift from its brown wrapping. "This book was written by a friend of mine, Robert Louis Stevenson. It is a work of genius!"

John Black accepted the package, withdrew the book, stroked its cover as if it were a baby bird, then quickly hid it under his shirt. "We're not allowed to accept gifts," he whispered.

"Well, you must have this book," Jamie said conspiratorially. "It is meant for you. Jim Hawkins is a brave boy, and you must be a brave boy too."

Just then the matron returned. "Time for you to be going, Mr. James," she said.

"Yes, madam, you are so right. Oh, and the boy has been complaining of a stomach cramp. Haven't you, John?"

The boy held the book close to his body with both arms and bent at the waist as if suffering from a severe stomach ache. "Yes, sir," he moaned softly.

"I think he needs bed rest right away, madam. Good-bye, John. I will write."

As soon as he reached his narrow cot and the matron had left the dormitory, the boy slipped the book beneath his bed's thin mattress, where he had long hidden the now shabby linen shawl that Themba had used to wrap him on her back so long ago, as well as the drawing pad and Crayons this Mr. James had given him the day before. No one — except his best friend Dougal — was to know of his hidden treasures.

On the train to Kirriemuir, James Barrie smiled. He'd just come up with a new, and, he felt, inspired plan. He would ask his second leading lady, Mary Ansell, to marry him. He was, after all, thirty-two years old now, and his closest friends were getting married. It was time. As everyone remarked to him, Mary was a particularly pretty girl, and she seemed to admire him. If he were a married man, he could adopt John Black as his own son. He, James Barrie, would be the hero! He would become the father of Helen's boy! What a happy ending to a sad, sad story! Helen would be so pleased! He could hardly sit still on the train's seat.

Jamie's glowing reports of his visits with young John Black were well received in Kirriemuir. Jane Ann passed the news to Agnes, who "thanked the good Lord" that the boy was being well cared for and well schooled at the Dean. "Some day I'll go an' visit him mysel'," she said weakly, knowing full well that that day would likely never come.

Some months later, after working up the courage, James Barrie quietly proposed to the pretty young actress Mary Ansell. He then suggested that soon after their wedding they could begin making arrangements to legally adopt the orphan boy he'd told her all about. Mary, who had long awaited Jamie's proposal, happily accepted his offer of marriage. She yearned to be the wife of the famous and prosperous James Matthew Barrie, to live in London near Kensington Gardens, and to be part of his social set. But she rejected out of hand the idea of adopting the orphan John Black.

"Oh, James," she said, laughing her light, theatrical laugh, "you know that would never work! Adopting a seven-year-old boy who was raised by Zulus? Just imagine our taking him with us to Vailima to visit your friend Stevenson! The little savage would likely run off with the Samoan natives!

"No, James. We will have children of our own! You'll see." With this, she smiled her most coquettish smile, tossed her pretty head, waved her slender right arm, and waltzed out of the room, as if exiting stage left.

Children of our own? Jamie fretted. But that would require carnal love....

James Barrie never again brought up the matter of adopting Helen's son with Mary. And he never again found the time in his busy schedule to visit John at the Dean Orphanage in Edinburgh.

Edinburgh, 1899

He had been waiting for this day for a long time. It was his nature to keep his own counsel, so he had told no one about his planned escape, not even Dougal, who was the closest he'd ever come to having a brother.

It had been nearly ten years since he was placed in this "charitable" home for orphaned or destitute children in Scotland's capital. Already, two-thirds of his life had been spent in what he considered to be a prison, despite its handsome façade. Yes, the massive, three-story stone building with its Greek columned portico was impressive to outsiders. Wealthy lady patrons were regularly invited to have tea on the front lawn; he would watch them from an upstairs window. But he well knew that those donors never ventured beyond the entryway. They were never witness to the truths inside.

These truths were cold and harsh in the extreme, he knew first-hand. Too often he'd seen children whipped for no apparent reason. He and his fellow orphans were fed only cold, lumpy porridge and limp, gray-green, overcooked kale most of the year. All of the children slept on thin, worn mattresses in overcrowded, under-heated dormitories. They were made to wear crude uniforms with the institution's name stamped on them, making their classmates at the local school see them as pariahs, and making the orphans themselves feel abandoned and worthless.

At times the shame of it had been almost too much for him to bear. And the cruelty, too. When he'd first arrived, he spoke little English. The older boys mocked him, taunting him and calling him names, such as *"Dumb kafir!"* and *"Albino Zulu!"* He said nothing to them in response; in fact, for a long time he chose not to speak at all. But in his heart, he yearned for Themba and the warm, soft embraces and kind, soothing, musical words of the Zulu women of his early childhood. At night, in the darkness, he would pull what remained of Themba's shawl from beneath his mattress and breath in the still-lingering, earthy scent of her skin.

Over the years at the orphanage he'd learned to walk tall and maintain a sense of quiet dignity, like the Zulu men he had been taught to emulate as a small boy. But it pained him to see other orphans treated cruelly. If a boy, for example, wet his bed in the night, he was forced to carry his soaked mattress until the urine dried. If a girl made a mistake in her knitting, she was made a laughingstock as her efforts were violently pulled to shreds for everyone to see.

One time, when John's friend Dougal wet his bed, he was made to stand outside all day the next day, with the mattress strapped to his back by a man's long leather belt, the mattress facing in the direction that the sun would be — if it were ever to emerge from behind the thick blanket of gray clouds. The soaking mattress made Dougal shiver. He grew so chilled and weary he could barely keep standing. The other boys mocked him and jeered, "Pissy-missy!" and "Look at the wee wet-the-bed, wet-the-bed" and nobody stopped them.

From that day on, Dougal told John, he slept with an old, found rag held tight to his penis, to catch any leaks in case he should once again dream he was a baby in a clean, soft, white nappy, free to pee.

Fortunately, John Black had never wet his bed in the night. If he had, the urine would surely have damaged his secret treasures, the old shawl and the gifts from that strange man who once came to visit him when he was young. What did the man call himself? "Uncle Jamie?" He had promised to write, but he never did. Or, perhaps, if he had, the headmaster or matron had confiscated his letters.

John Black had forgotten what that man looked like, but he never forgot the man's gifts. At every opportunity, the boy had stolen the chance to make small, colorful drawings in the blank pages of the artist's pad and to read his very own copy of *Treasure Island*. This book had become his bible, his inspiration, his salvation, and his guide for quietly, patiently planning his escape.

He'd read the book so many times he'd practically memorized short passages as though it were scripture.

The narrator, Jim Hawkins, "only a boy," had "made up his mind." He'd come up with a plan to "slip out when nobody was watching." When "the coast was clear," he "made a bolt for it over the stockade and into the thickest of the trees..."

Jim Hawkins escaped, so John Black knew that he would escape one day too.

He knew also that his escape — before he was forced out at fifteen, when he like the other orphan boys would be given only two choices in life, to become a servant to the wealthy or a soldier for the empire — was an act of rebellion and retribution. The headmaster would surely be called to account for the disappearance of yet another of the almost one hundred young inmates in the institution. Perhaps this time, John Black thought, the man would lose his job and be replaced by someone better, someone, perhaps, like the fabled Mr. Tod. *Good!*

This plan, this scheme, fueled by his reading and rereading of *Treasure Island,* was also an act of daring adventure. By now, he had been researching and rehearsing his getaway for half a lifetime. He felt confident in his ability to carry it out. Like young Jim Hawkins, the young John Black was determined to slip out when nobody was watching, with his pockets filled with hoarded biscuits, so he wouldn't starve. His mind was made up. He felt as if a powerful hand were guiding him to freedom and betterment, to a faraway place called Manhattan Island, his own Treasure Island.

This is how he flew away:

On a warm clear evening in June, in the summer of his fourteenth year, in the final year of the nineteenth century, after tucking his treasured copy of *Treasure Island* under the mattress of Dougal's bed while his friend slept soundly, the young John Black quietly crept off, climbed the iron fence to the old cemetery next door, and hid there until summer-twilight nightfall, seemingly protected by all the long-since-departed souls. Then he tiptoed into the nearby old mill village in the valley by the Water of Leith and followed the winding water's path to the port. This route was slow, slippery, muddy, overhung by moss and trees, filled with night sounds and frightening at times; but it was sure.

Whenever the cloud cover broke, he stopped to study the stars, searching for the one that looked like fire. He knew that star would lead him to the sea, where, in the new day, he would hide away on a ship bound for New York and freedom.

It never crossed his mind that he might fail.

When, in the early hours of the morning, he saw a seagull overhead, swooping and squawking as if celebrating the boy's own successful flight, he knew he was close. The seaport was less than a mile away.

A port at the time of a vessel's near-departure is a busy, noisy, smelly, crowded scene. As Helen herself had experienced seventeen years before, Leith's cobblestone streets clattered with the wheels of pushcarts, barrows, and carriages, as well as men's boots, ladies' heels, and horses' hooves. The damp, still air smelled of dead fish and brine.

Ticket-holding passengers and their well-wishing friends and family huddled in clusters on the docks, lace-trimmed handkerchiefs pressed to their noses, only noticing one another, as if for the last time. Ship officials in smart blue uniforms, too busy to look up, studied lists and shouted orders. Burly dockworkers, with eyes only for their loads, hoisted heavy cargo as though it were bales of cotton. Vendors hawked food and beverages. Babies cried.

White seagulls swooped and squawked in the morning sky in great numbers now. They alone saw the boy slip past the crowds. Their squawking sounded jubilant, like haughty, conspiratorial laughter.

He was a thin boy, adept at squeezing into narrow crevices to try to disappear. He was a Zulu hunter, stealthy, silent, and observant as a hawk. He was young Jim Hawkins on the adventure of a lifetime. His teeth were clenched. He told himself he was not afraid.

His early years in Africa had instilled in him a quiet patience and resilience. His almost ten years of incarceration at the orphanage had fostered in him a growing determination to break free. On this day, despite his hunger and thirst and the loud hammering of his heart in his thin, frail ribcage, despite his muddied shoes, his torn trousers and tattered cardigan, and his sore arm from clinging so tightly to the remaining treasures he held close to his body, he managed to make his way onto the ship at Leith harbor undetected. As though he were only a ghost.

Atlantic Ocean, Summer 1899

The middle-aged Scottish businessman liked to walk the decks early in the morning. He called it his "constitutional." He'd leave his wife still sleeping in their stateroom bedroom, don his dark suit, coat and hat, and walk briskly, head high, taking it all in. He fancied himself an explorer and the ship a sparsely habited island in a vast, unbroken ocean, beneath a curdled-milk sky. This was his first transatlantic voyage, and it seemed to bring out the latent poet-adventurer in him.

Then early one morning not long after leaving port, before the sun had woken fully and neither passengers nor crew had found their way on deck, the man taking his constitutional looked down and noticed something strange: a muddy old leather shoe sticking out from under a pile of sacking in a dark corner near a steam pipe. The man stopped abruptly to take a better look. His explorer's heart raced. *What had he discovered? A dead body? A crime scene? What a find!*

He approached the lump of jute sacks and patted it. It jumped. Then a dirty, boney hand emerged and a tussled, sandy-haired head peeked out like a terrified young animal from its dark cave.

The man bent lower to take a better look. "Son," he said when he saw the boy, "are you all right?"

The boy couldn't answer. *Son? No one had ever called him by that name. Why was this stranger calling him "Son"? And what did "all right" mean? What did "all right" feel like?* If he had ever been "all right," he'd forgotten the feeling. He couldn't understand the man's language, even though by now the boy spoke English well. He looked at the man in frightened, mute confusion.

"Come," the man said, reaching his arms out to the boy to help him up. "Let's talk. I won't hurt you." He removed his coat and wrapped it around the boy's thin shoulders. "You're cold," the man said. "When was the last time you had a bath and a meal?"

The boy still couldn't answer. He didn't know. *A bath? My last cold shower in the outdoor washhouse at the orphanage was many days ago. And a meal? On a plate? Do stale stolen biscuits count as a meal?* He shook his head.

"Let's sit here," the man said, guiding the trembling boy to a long wooden bench, sitting beside him on the right, wrapping his left arm around him for warmth and protection, as well as to prevent him from running away.

"What is your name, son?" The man studied the boy's face and his darkly circled blue-green eyes. The boy wasn't well, he could see; he was starved and dehydrated, and he smelled as though he hadn't bathed in days. But the man didn't pull away; something about the boy's face intrigued him. It looked familiar to him, as if he'd seen it somewhere, somehow, before.

"Black, sir. John Black, sir."

"James Wilkie from Kirriemuir, Angus," the man said, which gave the boy a jolt. The man held out his large, smooth right hand and enclosed the boy's thin right hand in his.

Kirriemuir? the boy thought. Kirriemuir? Could he be imagining this? Were there more than one Kirriemuirs in Scotland? Was he still huddled under the jute sacks, dreaming?

"And where are *you* from, John?"

"I've just left an orphanage, sir, in Edinburgh. Please don't send me back, sir." The boy clenched both of his hands together in his lap. His knuckles were blue-white.

Wilkie slapped his own thigh with his right hand. "I wouldn't think of it, laddie! No! I wouldn't do that to you. We're not going *backward,* we're going *forward!*" With sudden gusto, the man motioned in the direction the ship was heading. "You're on an adventure —"

The boy raised his head and nodded, buoyed by the man's enthusiasm.

"— and I'm an adventurer, too! What's life without a few risks, I say! We're in this together, John Black! Now let's go have a nice breakfast with my wife."

The boy gripped his stomach, still holding tight to his treasures.

The food was rich, richer than the boy had ever eaten —softly scrambled eggs made with heavy cream, crisply cooked bacon, thickly sliced toast slathered with real butter and marmalade, crumbly scones studded with currants, sweetened coffee mixed with an equal measure of hot, foamy milk. He ate and drank slowly, savoring every mouthful, his head spinning, still feeling as if he were dreaming.

Mrs. Wilkie sat with them at the table in the couple's private stateroom picking at her food and fanning her face. The boy smelled, she'd complained to her husband privately. Why had he taken this beggar-boy in? Why, he could be a thief! He could be diseased! "Why didn't you ask my permission?" she'd demanded. Her husband turned a deaf ear to her complaints.

"John Black is a common name," the man said kindly to the boy. "There must be thousands of John Blacks all over the world at this very minute. Do you know where your people come from, John?"

"Kirriemuir, sir," the boy said.

With that, Mrs. Wilkie dropped her fork. James Wilkie nodded, as if this information came as no surprise.

"I don't believe him!" Mrs. Wilkie stormed. "He's only saying this because you told him we're from Kirriemuir! The boy is a beggar and a *liar!*"

With that, the boy opened his cardigan and pulled from it one of his treasures, what was left of the tattered linen shawl. The piece still somewhat intact included the corner embroidered with the now-faint words, *Helen David of Kirriemuir.* "This was my mother's," the boy said, without specifying which mother he meant.

Mrs. Wilkie gasped.

"They told me at the orphanage that my only living relative, my grandmother Agnes David of Kirriemuir, died last year at the age of 72," the boy said, words spilling from him as if a dam had broken. "She had been too old and infirm to take me in, sir. When my parents died in Natal, my grandmother thought the Dean Orphanage would take better care of me than she could. That's what they told me, sir. I never met her. I've never been to Kirriemuir. It's just a word to me, sir, nothing more."

Mrs. Wilkie dabbed her mouth with a linen napkin, then quickly dabbed her eyes. "Kirriemuir is a lovely little town, John," she said softly, now penitent. "We have lived there for many, many years. My husband's father, David Wilkie, and his uncle started the J&D Wilkie linen factory there in 1868."

"I knew of your grandmother Agnes, John," Mr. Wilkie added. "And I knew your parents, too, before they emigrated. Yes, Kirriemuir is indeed a small town — with a long memory."

The boy's skin tingled. He looked up from his plate of half-eaten scrambled eggs, open-mouthed, like a baby bird. He had no memories of his Scottish parents. He knew little about them, only what that little man had tried to tell him so long ago. His parents were fictional characters to him.

"Your mother Helen worked at my linen factory, and your father William was a clerk at the railway station next door. She was considered the most beautiful girl in Kirriemuir. Spirited. And talented, too. She sang like a nightingale. And he was a tall, handsome, artistic lad —"

John Black withdrew from his shirt the last of his hidden treasures, his drawing pad and crayons, given to him so long ago by that strange visitor to the orphanage.

"I like to draw," the boy said.

Mrs. Wilkie drew a long, deep breath. "Oh, what a *coincidence* that we should meet like this!" she sighed.

"Not a coincidence at all, my dear," her husband corrected her. "Surely it is God's hand at work.

The Wilkies, on holiday from Scotland to visit one of James Wilkie's relations who had emigrated to Morristown, New Jersey, took the boy John Black under their wing for the duration of the voyage. They fed him, found suitable clothing for him, and allowed him to sleep on the sofa in the parlor of their stateroom. Mr. Wilkie used his considerable influence to see that the boy wasn't punished for stowing away. He paid for John's passage and promptly dispatched with the U.S. Immigration Bureau's paperwork. In effect, if not officially, the Wilkies adopted the boy and walked proudly with him when they disembarked, completely bypassing the dreaded inspectors waiting to scrutinize the ship's lower classes of passengers on Ellis Island.

Taos, New Mexico, Summer 2012

My grandfather John Black was just one of the nearly quarter million immigrants to arrive at Ellis Island in New York harbor in the year 1899. He was no longer alone, no longer an orphan. The Wilkie family in Morristown, New Jersey, took the boy in and cared for him like a son. The Wilkies saw that he got an education and later had him apprenticed to a trade. He became a successful entrepreneur, starting his own business as a painting contractor. He found his portion of treasure.

Like his parents, whom he never knew, the quiet young man also found his personal self-expression in painting and singing.

He was famous in Morristown, I've been told, for singing favorite Scottish and Irish ballads at Masonic gatherings. Whenever he began singing, in his deeply resonant baritone, "Oh, Danny boy, the pipes, the pipes are calling, from glen to glen and down the mountainside — the summer's gone, and all the roses falling," the roomful of immigrants was silent except for the sniffling.

I didn't know him well (we didn't visit often), nor for very long (he died of a heart attack at the age of sixty-nine, when I was nine), but I loved and admired Helen's son, our grandfather, "Pop," greatly. I own only one, old, black-and-white photo of him, which I framed and placed on a windowsill altar I recently made to Helen. This altar includes several white candles, some framed pressed flowers I picked in Kirriemuir, the small chunk of red sandstone I took from a crumbling ancient wall there, and my photo of the view from the top of Hill Cemetery.

In the professionally taken black-and-white photo, Pop is a fair-haired young man in his mid-twenties wearing a dark suit, white shirt and narrow tie, sitting above and slightly behind his pretty, young, Scottish wife Jessie. Jessie's dark hair is full and upswept; her long-sleeved dress has a high collar and a fitted, tiny waist. The two, attractive by anyone's estimation, look intently at the camera with slight, closed-mouthed smiles.

My most vivid memory of Pop dates to the time of my youngest sister's birth, over sixty years ago. I was five, and my other sister was three. My younger sister and I were left with Pop and his second wife Nellie (a Scotswoman he'd married after Jessie's death from cancer) at Pop's three-story, white clapboard home on Western Avenue in Morristown while my mother was in the hospital giving birth.

Somehow I had managed to follow Pop like a silent shadow up the staircase that led to his "secret studio" in the attic. There, I discovered he had created an artist's atelier for himself, with a paint-spattered wooden easel in the center of the room; wooden side tables littered with crumpled, silver tubes of oil paints and jars filled with bouquets of paint brushes of all sizes; and canvasses leaning like fallen dominoes at the far ends of the floor, where it was too low for Pop, a tall, slim man, to stand.

He showed me his completed paintings, conspiratorially, as if he were too shy to exhibit them elsewhere, as if they were a secret that had to remain between him and me. Each one of them was of a massive ship rocked by roiling blue seas. Curiously, the ships that Pop painted were not like the steamships he had traveled on when he was a boy — on his way from South Africa to the orphanage in Edinburgh, and, later, as a stowaway, from Britain bound for Ellis Island. Pop's paintings were of older, many-masted sailing ships, like the ones in *Treasure Island*.

Postscript

Novelist and dramatist James Matthew Barrie of Kirrie-muir, Scotland, whose timeless, world-renowned play *Peter Pan* was first produced in 1904, was made a baronet by King George V of England in 1913. He and his wife, the actress Mary Ansell, were married for fifteen years, but they never had children; reportedly, their relationship was never consummated. She left him for a younger man in 1908, and she and Barrie were divorced the following year.

J. M. Barrie died of pneumonia in London in 1937 at the age of 77 and is buried beside his parents and siblings in the Hill Cemetery in Kirriemuir. Unlike Helen, he came home.

Acknowledgments

In the nearly ten years since I began research for this work of historical fiction, reading everything I could whenever I could on late-nineteenth-century Scottish and South African history, as well as J. M. Barrie's early novels and several biographies of Barrie, I've sometimes felt I was living in the nineteenth century and the young James Barrie was one of my close friends. Among the wonderful books and authors I must thank for this magic are:

J. M. Barrie: The Man Behind the Image, by Janet Dunbar; *J. M. Barrie and the Lost Boys*, by Andrew Birkin; *The Story of J. M. B.: A Biography*, by Denis Mackail; *A History of Scotland*, by J. D. Mackie; *A Century of the Scottish People: 1830-1950*, by T. C. Smout; and *My African Home: Bush Life in Natal*, by Eliza Whigham Feilden.

When I was living in Taos, a particularly literary little town in the mountains of northern New Mexico, and teaching English and Creative Writing at UNM-Taos, a number of friends and UNM colleagues read early drafts of this novel and offered invaluable help, feedback and encouragement. Among them were: Jennifer Acampora, Tania Casselle, Teresa Dovalpage, Judith Kendall, Linda Michel-Cassidy, Margery Reading, Jeremy McDonald (UNM Art Dept.), and Ana Pacheco (UNM Library).

Friends farther afield also shared their thoughts and opinions on various stages of the manuscript, for which I'm deeply grateful. They are: Morgan Case, Belmont Freeman, John Ricca, Davida Singer, Iris Staenberg, Fiona Timms, Wendy Tyson, and Paulette Valliere.

I was, alas, not able to visit nineteenth-century Natal, South Africa, in person, so I had to rely on local historians' help online. For their generous and patient assistance, I am especially indebted to Brian Kaighin at Ladysmith History and Michael Cottrell, Archivist at KwaZulu-Natal Railway Society. David Mahler in the Encyclopedia Britannica's Editorial Department was immensely helpful in digging into early editions of their encyclopedias to share with me what Jamie Barrie learned about Natal at that time.

I did visit Scotland in the summer of 2011 and was happy to see that it hasn't changed all that much since Helen and William's day. Thanks to the digitized records at the ScotlandsPeople Centre, part of the National Archives of Scotland (General Register House, 2 Princes Street, Edinburgh — www.nas.gov.uk), I was able to gather basic information from birth, marriage, and census records about Helen and Will and their respective families and to learn that their home town was Kirriemuir. But before traveling to Kirrie, I visited the Dean Gallery in Edinburgh, once the Dean Orphanage, and spoke with an enormously knowledgeable and helpful young employee there, Mhairi Scott, who shared with me stories she'd learned about life at the orphanage from its aged former "inmates" who'd returned to the Dean as tourists.

In Kirriemuir I felt as if I'd come home. Everyone I met who learned of my quest, opened their arms and hearts to me. Among the names I made note of: Joyce Millar, Ian Sangster, and the Rev. Malcolm Rooney of the Old Parish Church. David Clark, owner of the Thrums Hotel on Bank Street, put me in touch with his friend David G. Orr, a local historian, who dropped whatever he'd been planning to do that morning to take me on a walking tour of Kirrie – showing me, in particular, where Helen had worked at the Wilkie Linen Factory and where Will had worked as a clerk at the railway station.

Matthew Whatley, the young proprietor of Whatley's Bookshop (now, sadly, closed) phoned his friend, the historian and J. M. Barrie aficionado, Sandra Afflek (author of *A Guide to Kirriemuir & District* and *The Little Red Town & JMB*), who rushed in to help me. On another walking tour, this one into the cool summer evening twilight, Sandra showed me where Will, Helen and Jamie went to school and church together and where they no doubt lived as neighbors.

"Do you think it's crazy of me to be pursuing this," I asked Sandra on the way back to my hotel, "and my needing to write about their lives — even though I know so little?"

"No, not at all," she told me earnestly, "in fact, you *must* do so." And she has been cheering me on in this pursuit ever since.

I am immensely grateful to Sandra for all that she has done to help make this book a reality.

Finally, without the enormous talents of my dear friends Barbara L. Scott and Rebecca Lenzini of Nighthawk Press in Taos, this beautiful book would still be waiting to be born. I cannot thank them enough.

Bonnie Lee Black
San Miguel de Allende
Mexico
May 2018

About the Author

Bonnie Lee Black is the author of the memoir *Somewhere Child* (Viking Press, 1981; now available as an eBook), which was instrumental in the creation of the National Center for Missing and Exploited Children. Her second memoir, about her U.S. Peace Corps service in Gabon, Central Africa, *How to Cook a Crocodile* (Peace Corps Writers, 2010), won a "Best in the World" award from Gourmand International in Paris in 2012. The manuscript for her Mali memoir, *How to Make an African Quilt: The Story of the Patchwork Project of Ségou, Mali*, won first place in the memoir-book category in the SouthWest Writers Annual Writing Contest, 2011.

Black earned a bachelor of arts degree with honors from Columbia University in New York in 1979 and an MFA in Creative Writing from Antioch University-Los Angeles in 2007. She worked as a professional writer and editor in New York City for twenty years and has been an educator in the United States and overseas for more than twenty years. Her essays have appeared in a number of published anthologies and literary journals.

She lived in Taos, New Mexico, and taught English and Creative Writing at UNM-Taos for more than ten years. In 2012 she was chosen one of the Remarkable Women of Taos and was featured in a book by the same title, compiled and edited by the late Elizabeth Cunningham. Now retired and living in San Miguel de Allende, Mexico, she writes an award-winning weekly blog called "The WOW Factor — Words of Wisdom from Wise Older Women": *www.bonnieleeblack.com/blog/*.

For more information on the author, visit her website at *www.bonnieleeblack.com.*

www.ingramcontent.com/pod-product-compliance
Lightning Source LLC
Chambersburg PA
CBHW022008100426
42736CB00041B/1039